A World of Old and New Water Issues

Also from Westphalia Press

westphaliapress.org

A World of Old and New Water Issues

Volume 2, Number 2 of New Water Policy and Practice

Edited by Jeff Camkin & Susana Neto

WESTPHALIA PRESS
An imprint of Policy Studies Organization

A World of Old and New Water Issues: Volume 2, Number 2 of New Water Policy and Practice
All Rights Reserved © 2016 by Policy Studies Organization

Westphalia Press
An imprint of Policy Studies Organization
1527 New Hampshire Ave., NW
Washington, D.C. 20036
info@ipsonet.org

ISBN-13: 978-1-63391-731-6
ISBN-10: 1633917312

Cover design by Jeffrey Barnes:
www.jbarnesbook.design

Daniel Gutierrez-Sandoval, Executive Director
PSO and Westphalia Press

Updated material and comments on this edition
can be found at the Westphalia Press website:
www.westphaliapress.org

Table of Contents

Editorial Welcome

A World of Old and New Water Issues

Welcome to the fourth issue of *New Water Policy and Practice Journal: A Platform for the World's Emerging Water Leaders and Thinkers.*

One of our main aims at New Water Policy and Practice Journal is to support emerging water leaders and thinkers to develop and share their ideas on how to address the varied challenges for water management around the world. In our first three issues we have already had papers from 14 different countries—Angola, Australia, Canada, China, Equador, India, Indonesia, Israel, Laos, Malaysia, Pakistan, Portugal, South Africa and the United States.

In this fourth edition we have an eclectic suite of papers which demonstrate the great diversity of challenges in water management, and the opportunities that exist by sharing experiences.

Leading the way is Prof Shahbaz Khan, Regional Director of UNESCO for Asia and the Pacific Region and a member of the NWPP International Advisory Board. In his Opinion Editorial, Shahbaz discusses the paradigm shift that is needed in water management, framed around Agenda 2030 and the Sustainable Development Goals. He identifies the key water challenges of the twenty-first century and discusses important directions, including dealing with the complexity and inter-relatedness of the challenges, ensuring water as a human right, putting water management in the hands of women (who are often the users of water but with low participation in decision-making), and increasing human capacity in water management.

In the first paper, Alex Gardner and Jeanette Hanson from the University of Western Australia and the Cooperative Research Centre for Water Sensitive Cities, Australia, then take a look at the legal duties to restore wetlands and waterways, including by the provision of environmental water flows, under international and national law in Australia.

Jorge Gonçalves, Davit Asanidze, and Pedro Pinto, researchers with the Technical University of Lisbon, then take us to Tbilisi, Georgia, with a look through the riverfront mirror to the transformations in post-Soviet cities, finding it representative of the challenges faced by cities that experienced the fast transition from state-controlled to open-market economies.

doi: 10.18278/nwpp.2.2.1

We then switch gears with José Javier Serrano, whose paper explores the impact of art in social movements aiming to protect water resources from the pressures of Coal Seam Gas development. Completed as part of a Master course in Integrated Water Management, the paper follows some of the activities of the "Lock the Gate Alliance" which encourages policy changes to stop CSG activities unless they are proven safe for the environment, water and land resources, and human health.

The fourth paper in this edition comes from the European Union-funded Transbasin project, a collaboration of researchers from Israel, Palestine, Jordan and Portugal. With the occupied Palestinian territories as a case study, the multinational team of authors, Sara Boavida, Mafalda Pinto, Teresa Salvador, Monther Hind and Susana Neto, considers centralized versus decentralized wastewater systems and the potential for water reuse to help resolve water sharing issues in one of the world's most complex transboundary contexts.

We hope you enjoy this latest journey through the challenging world of water management.

With our very best wishes.
Jeff Camkin and Susana Neto
Editors-in-Chief

Opinion Editorial: Sustainable Development Goal 6 and Agenda 2030—A Paradigm Shift in Water Management to Realise the Future We Want for All

Shahbaz Khan[A,B]

Background

Agenda 2030 provides both the vision and the commitment to address and resolve the big issues of our time, including: poverty eradication, peace and security, safe and sufficient food, sustainable energy, pollution prevention and control, water and environmental resources management, disease control, mobility, natural and man-induced disasters, population growth, urbanization, and sustainable/liveable cities. The development of solutions to these key global challenges and the overall transition towards a green economy will need to be based on sound science, technology, and innovation. Water plays a key role in almost all the global challenges and therefore water-related Sustainable Development Goal 6 (SDG 6) is an enabling goal for the Agenda 2030.

There are many challenges that modern society is facing in terms of water management (Box 1). The poorest people, mostly women, are suffering the greatest scarcity and deterioration of water quality. This situation is exacerbated by factors such as climate change, the increasing intensification of farming and agriculture, as well as increasing demand on water as a result of population growth and changing lifestyles. On the other hand, in many instances water management policies and practices have ignored the needs of the people who in a daily routine have to face water scarcity, and therefore must design new adaptive strategies to meet their needs. One of the targets of the Millennium Development Goals (MDGs) was to halve the proportion of the population without sustainable access to safe drinking water between 2000 and 2015. We are still facing several barriers to reach this objective. One of the handicaps is the dissemination of paradigms and technologies developed under differing socio-cultural setting in developed countries to solve water challenges in the developing countries. As a result these are not always accepted or fully incorporated, and even sometimes they become a source of conflict or produce negative effects on the target groups and their ecosystems. Besides, there are other pressing water issues beyond water supply and sanitation that need to be addressed urgently (Box 1). This is the time to create

[A] Regional Director of UNESCO for Asia and the Pacific Region and UNESCO

[B] New Water Policy and Practice International Advisory Board

doi: 10.18278/nwpp.2.2.2

new ways to approach water issues in the Agenda 2030 era. We must create a real water democracy, promoted from the grassroots which is inclusive and participatory in policies and practices. This new movement must listen to different voices and knowledge, and then add and converge to find common and better solutions for everyone.

Box 1. Key Water Challenges

The Post-2015 Development Agenda needs to respond to new global water realities, which indicate that humanity is facing numerous unprecedented and inter-connected socio-economic and environmental sustainability challenges further complicated by an intensifying hydrological cycle under global change. The most pressing water challenges of the twenty-first century include:

- Intensifying water efficiencies in food production
- Failing access to water and sanitation
- Stressed aquatic ecosystems and biodiversity loss
- Increasing conflicts on water rights
- Degrading water quality
- Ever increasing human water foot prints
- Unsustainable groundwater abstractions
- Frequent hydrologic extreme events causing floods and droughts
- Water privatization leading to inequalities in water access
- Closed rivers and over exploited aquifer systems leading to water stress for all uses
- Unplanned urban growth threatening water balances
- Inadequate human and institutional capacities to deal with the above-mentioned challenges.

Complexities and Inter-Relatedness of Water Challenges

These water-related global challenges are hugely complex with strong inter-connections. For instance, ensuring food security for a rapidly growing world population depends on availability of water, land and energy, and also on scientific breakthroughs in enhancing production. Current food production methods, however, are highly polluting, causing eutrophication, greenhouse gas emissions, biodiversity loss, and water stress. In addition, climate change and extreme weather events lead to massive crop damage and pose a growing threat to agriculture yields and food security. The task to address the above-mentioned water challenges is phenomenally complex, and therefore science has to play a major role in helping to understand the complexities and multidimensional character of sustainable development.

Ensuring Water as a Human Right

On July 28, 2010, through Resolution 64/292, the United Nations General Assembly explicitly recognized the human right to water and sanitation and acknowledged that clean drinking water and sanitation are essential to the realisation of all human rights. Water democracy comes from political democracy enabling the availability of water, making possible that the water is "everybody's business." This is a matter of right to water and life. There is a need to understand economic and legislative aspects of providing water and sanitation as a human right in different hydrogeographical and societal settings. The human right to water has to entitle everyone to sufficient, safe, acceptable, physically accessible, and affordable water for personal and domestic uses. A rights-based approach is needed to prioritize non-discriminatory access to water, promote inclusive participation in all decision-making mechanisms, and ensure accountability and legal obligations of public institutions.

Water Security beyond Water Supply and Sanitation Goals

MDG 7, Target 7c, focuses on the importance of providing safe drinking water and sanitation. But, there are additional water issues beyond Target 7c that also need attention. Water is the main limiting factor preventing increased food production, water quality deterioration affects biodiversity, and many people (especially children) die from water-borne disease. It is estimated that over 90% of all climate change impact is water related; we need better flood forecasting, community preparedness, and adaptation measures. The rivers and groundwater systems are becoming increasingly polluted; this creates challenges to society at large for aquifer and river restoration and integrated water resources management. There is an urgent need to go beyond MDG Target 7c, by understanding ecological impacts of water projects, including for drinking water supply, but also for industrial water use, irrigation, and dams and dikes, on water quantity, quality, and related environment links.

More Crop Per Drop

More than 70% of all water use globally goes to food production. To secure sufficient food production for an estimated 9 billion people in 2050, we need to consider a paradigm shift in the way we produce food. There are medium (3–5 years) and longer term (beyond 5 years) challenges to achieve societal benefits through more crop per drop in water stressed regions. These objectives are:

- Medium term: improve efficiencies (drought resistant crops, high yield/low water use varieties via biotech; efficiency of irrigation systems; etc.)
- Longer term: new ways of food production with full water and nutrient recycle (on the extreme end of the scale there is the option to produce meat in factories).

Water Culture a Sound Basis for Water Management

Water is life because, "there is no life without water," the existence of every society is about the existence of a determined culture of water. There is no society or social group without water culture, every community has its own water values. Every society and every social group has developed a unique water culture, allowing them to live in their territory. Moreover, if we want to change a culture of water into another, this requires necessarily restructuring of the modes of perception, the belief systems, and the ways to perceive, to believe, to know, to organize, to live, and to plan a common future. We have to build bridges with the past and the present to build better water futures. It is from culture that we can produce a real process of change towards a sustainable development.

Adaptive Water Management for Better Coping with Extremes

Climate change affects both the quality and availability of water resources. The consequences are significant. Water-related natural disasters, such as flooding, drought, and landslides, are becoming more frequent and more severe. Rising temperatures, causing increased evaporation and glacial melt, are reducing the reliability and quality of water supplies. Responsible management of water must take into account the real danger of physical water renewability, which not only depends on global climate change (which affects the water cycle in quantitative terms), but also on the local regional and global water management practices. In many parts of the world both the quantity and good-quality water are on substantial decline. The main pollutants of groundwater are nitrates that are generated primarily by intensive farming and agricultural fertilizers and pesticides. Adaptive water management is needed to adjust practices in accordance with anticipated climate change impacts on water resources, to use the limited water efficiently and manage the agriculture water productivity effectively by making every drop counts for social, economic, and environmental benefits to society and nature.

Inclusive and Relevant Water Technologies to Avoid Unintended Consequences

Imported and exclusive technological models which were elaborated under different environmental and cultural conditions can sometimes have negative impacts on both environment and society. For example, reservoirs that apart from having a huge impact at social and environmental level can have a limited life because they rapidly accumulate sediments if constructed in unstable watersheds. 100% of the public water supply is treated to make it drinkable while the drinking, food cooking, and water washing uses account for less than 35%. This means that 65% of the work and energy used is not necessary. Another example is the use of chlorine. This is used to prevent microbes to proliferate along the way in the supply network, but at the same time it creates new health concerns, producing several toxic compounds, some of them recognized as carcinogenic. Besides, the toxicity of chlorine, it requires a lot of energy to be produced. In some areas the impact of the exploitation of underground aquifers is usually gradual and "invisible." The rate of exploitation of aquifer systems is unsustainable in most areas and can cause irrecoverable land subsidence. The excessive exploitation of coastal aquifers is causing sea water intrusion. There is a need for new forms of technology and innovation as well as improved applications for using different sources of water (such as rain water harvesting, untreated river water, and grey water reuse) fit for purpose.

Paradigm Shift in Urban Water Management

Urbanization is keeping domestic water use on an upward trend. Today an average person uses more than double the water than a hundred years before. Domestic water use represents on average 11% of total water withdrawal worldwide and is used to supply towns, cities, and rural communities (the vast majority of domestic water consumption is linked to the hygiene). The natural hydrological processes are significantly changed by new built environment. In addition, rainwater collects chemicals and other concentrated forms of pollutant (such as zinc and lead), which are then carried directly into streams and rivers. Rainwater is discharged with no prior treatment, especially in emerging and the least developed regions. In developing countries, more than 80% of wastewater is currently discharged into the environment in an untreated state, polluting rivers, lakes, and coastal areas. There is a need for formulating sound policies through learning alliances at different levels aimed at incorporating reduce, recycle, reuse, and redesign concepts in water-intensive foods and goods systems to reduce human water foot prints.

Management Needs to be in the Hands of Women

Women are often the primary users of water in domestic consumption, subsistence agriculture, health, and sanitation. Women in many cases also take the primary role in educating children, in child and family health, including sanitation, and in caring for the sick. They also spend a disproportionate number of hours on labour-intensive, time-consuming, and unpaid domestic tasks such as fetching water and firewood, washing clothes and dishes, and preparing meals. Too often, women and girls are disproportionately affected by the lack of access to water and, although women carry out most of the water-related tasks, play a key role in food production, especially in subsistence farming, their participation in decision-making processes on water and food management remains very low. This does not only result in biased and misinformed decision making, but also it jeopardizes the achievement of women's human rights, reducing their opportunities to education, decent work, and political engagement, and perpetuates the intergenerational transfer of poverty and disempowerment. Understanding gender roles can help plan water interventions and policies which are based on the knowledge of how and why people make the choices they do in water use in order to meet their needs.

Towards a New Hydro-Diplomacy for Crossing Water Boundaries

It is well known that water is not distributed equally among different sectors of society and across geopolitical boundaries. The problem of water is vital in all communities; no life or production is possible without water. The use of water, whether it is abundant or not, entails the real possibility of confrontations between social actors. Consequently, before we deal with water, it is necessary to picture the set of tensions that could be generated around it while crossing boundaries. The source of stress may be at local, regional, national, or international level. This is due to different positions adopted by individuals based on their subjectivity, which is the result of their cultures and their own relationship with water. The water sharing and use proposals have to include all agents in a major and constructive role. It is necessary to remember that all positions are worthy of consideration and if there is a real interest in establishing communication channels, it will be possible to converge and complement each other. Trying to put yourself in someone else's place and looking through their worldview, trying to discover how the other perceive the situation, is the first step in a process to reach water agreements.

Corporate Social Responsibility of the Water Businesses

In countries where many people lack access to safe water, the growth in bottled water consumption is dramatic, for example, by 50% a year in India. The global bottled water business is in the hands of a few multinational companies. The fact that a few companies can exploit very high-quality water for their own benefit while leaving behind social and ecological issues is questioned. Only a few companies own safe drinking water technologies that a local municipality can hardly assume. Also, the water extraction, which is often done in the higher parts of the mountains, in places of great natural value and landscape, creates a huge environmental impact as well as ecological impacts of associated packaging. In addition, bottled water requires transportation, which includes developing infrastructures such as roads, increasing fuel consumption, and emission of greenhouse gases. In meeting the drinking water challenges, there is a need for greater corporate and social responsibility of the private sector especially the multinational companies.

Increasing Human Capacities in All Water Management Areas

The key objective of integrated water resources management (IWRM) is to re-establish water quality and ecosystem functions through improved storm water management, human and industrial waste management, flood loss reduction, sedimentation and pollution control, improvement of water quality, recreation, education, and introduction of natural or manmade cropping systems tailored to deliver solutions at the river basin level. This needs to be set in a human rights-based approach aimed at achieving "sufficient, safe, acceptable, and affordable water for personal and domestic uses" for all. Locally appropriate IWRM-based formal and informal education at all levels is needed to address water supply and sanitation-related exclusion issues that are commonly rooted in weak governance, power inequality, and poverty, rather than sheer physical availability of water.

New Water Policy and Practice - Volume 2, Number 2 - Spring 2016

Legal Duties for Restoration of Waterways and Wetlands[A]

Alex Gardner[B,C] and Jeanette Jensen[B, C]

Many waterways and wetlands in south-west Australia require significant restoration, including environmental water allocations to assure adequate flows of water. Flows diminished by decades of consumptive uses have dwindled dramatically with climate change. Restoration aspirations are more likely to be achieved if there are binding legal duties on public agencies to undertake restoration. While such a duty exists internationally, it does not nationally. We propose how this may be remedied.

Keywords*: climate change, environmental law, Ramsar Convention, water allocation*

Implications for Practice:

- *Legal duties to restore wetlands and waterways can mandate decisions on environmental flows in water resource decision making.*
- *The Ramsar Convention framework expresses an international duty to maintain the ecological character of wetlands by provision of environmental water flows, which includes restoration of flows.*
- *Australian national water policy mandates statutory recognition of environmental flows, but the national Ramsar legislation does not.*
- *The Western Australian legislation neither implements the international duty nor complies with national water policy.*
- *Legislated national and state duties to maintain the ecological character of wetlands could create political expectations for restoration and mandate restoration decisions.*

[A] Alex Gardner and Jeanette Jensen conceived and wrote the article together, with Jeanette contributing the majority of the international legal discussion.

[B] Faculty of Law, The University of Western Australia, 35 Stirling Highway, Crawley, Australia

[C] The Cooperative Research Centre for Water Sensitive Cities

doi: 10.18278/nwpp.2.2.3

Introduction

In Australia, waterways and wetlands are mostly public resources managed by state governments under broad statutory authority that also provides for regulation of private rights in respect of water resources. Yet many of these waterways and wetlands require significant ecological restoration. We argue that there will be better prospects of achieving restoration aspirations if there are binding public legal duties on relevant public agencies to undertake and demonstrate the restoration.

Those legal duties can be expressed at the international and national (or domestic) levels. In international law, obligations create political expectations that are the foundation of international cooperation and can also facilitate domestic legal authority. In domestic law, public legal duties create political expectations that can influence executive government action. If those legal duties are effectively expressed, they will create justiciable obligations that can be enforced by proceedings for judicial review in a court of law.

An enforceable scheme of duties for waterways and wetlands restoration action may rest on three questions.

1. Is there a legal duty to restore waterways and wetlands by ensuring adequate water flow?
2. If so, what is the legal effect of decisions or instruments made in fulfillment of this duty, that is, are they binding on government agencies and all other persons?
3. Is there a duty on the responsible agencies to monitor and report on the implementation of the duty to restore?

In this article, we address only the first duty.

The water resources context for this legal analysis focuses on the quantity of water flows and the water-dependent ecosystem values, especially as the habitat of waterfowl. The need to preserve wetlands as waterfowl habitats was formally recognized internationally with the adoption of the *Convention on Wetlands of International Importance* (Ramsar Convention), which came into force in 1975. Since then, dams, diversions, and river management for human consumptive use have further reduced such flows significantly (Kingsford 2000). In southern Australia, the effects of those reduced water flows are being exacerbated by climate change-induced reductions in rainfall and streamflow (Bennet and Gardner 2014; Pittock et al. 2010). The global replication of these patterns led to the Ramsar Strategic Plan 2009–2015 identifying "the inadequate availability of water to wetlands" as the first of a number of issues causing continued deterioration and loss of wetlands (COP 2008a, Resolution X.1, p. 4).

The restoration of water flows for environmental purposes has been founded on the concept of "environmental water allocations" (EWAs), which aim to secure "*adequate* natural flows of water [...] to sustain streams, rivers, aquifers and estuaries, and their dependent ecosystems" (Gardner 2006, p. 208). Since 1996, Australian national water policy has recognized that the goal of EWAs is to both "sustain and where necessary *restore* ecological processes and biodiversity of water-dependent ecosystems" (ARMCANZ and ANZECC 1996, p. 5) [emphasis added]. It also declares that EWAs should be given statutory recognition, have the same degree of security as water access entitlements for consumptive use, and be fully accounted for (Gardner 2006; National Water Commission 2004).

The current law of Western Australia (WA) does not comply with national water policy and there is a history of breaching existing EWAs in order to supply water for human consumptive use (Bennett and Gardner 2014; Gardner 2006). There are 12 WA wetlands on the list of Wetlands of International Importance under the Ramsar Convention,[1] including the Peel-Harvey Estuary listed in 1990 (PHCC 2009). Four of the five major rivers that could deliver flows to the Estuary are dammed for consumptive use and the releases from them have dwindled dramatically in the drying climate. The Appendix shows the releases from the North Dandalup Dam for the period 2006–2007 to 2015–2016. Although the freshwater flow requirements of the Estuary are unknown, it is clear that the waterway flows to the Estuary are struggling (DoW 2012).

The WA Government is preparing water resources law reform (DoW 2015). Should that law mandate the restoration of environmental flows in a way that meets national water policy and fulfills our Ramsar Convention obligations? Does the Commonwealth Government have a duty to fulfill the Convention obligations in WA? We apply this first legal duty question to analyze an overview of the current regulatory framework applicable in WA—including the relevant international obligations and the Commonwealth and State legislation. *The Water Act 2007* (Cth) does not operate on wetlands management in WA.

The regulatory framework for restoration

We introduce the international, national, and state dimensions of this framework and then analyze each to ascertain whether it mandates restoration of waterways and wetlands by ensuring adequate water flow.

The most relevant international treaty is the Ramsar Convention, as the only convention dedicated to wetlands and waterfowl. It creates two essential obligations for Australia (Gardner 2012): (i) to designate for listing wetlands of international importance and to promote their conservation, and (ii) a general commitment to promote the wise use of all wetlands.[2]

The first obligation supports the Ramsar provisions of the *Environment Protection and Biodiversity Conservation Act 1999* (Cth) (*EPBC Act*) (Parts 3 and 15, Sub-Division B and Division 2, respectively.). The *EBPC Act* Ramsar provisions are directed only at specific conservation measures for listed wetlands. The States and Territories are seen as primarily responsible for the general implementation of both obligations for wetlands within their territory (Comino 1997).

---

[1] Government of Western Australia, Department of Parks and Wildlife, "Wetlands of national and international importance," on the Department's website, www.dpaw.wa.gov.au.

[2] There are other international agreements relevant to wetland management and migratory waterfowl, but they are outside the scope of this article. For example, there are the migratory bird agreements that Australia has with China, Korea, and Japan: Australian Government, Department of Environment, Migratory birds, http://www.environment.gov.au/biodiversity/migratory-species/migratory-birds#International_cooperation.

In WA, the two most relevant statutes that can directly regulate the flow of water in waterways and wetlands are the *Rights in Water and Irrigation Act 1914* (*RIWI Act*) and the *Environmental Protection Act 1986* (*EP Act*).

The Ramsar Convention

The Ramsar Convention does not include an explicit, general duty to restore. The obligations of Article 3.1 are the closest to such a duty.

> "The Contracting Parties shall formulate and implement their planning so as to promote the *conservation* of the wetlands included in the List, and as far as possible the wise use of wetlands in their territory." [emphasis added]

The obligation to "promote conservation" relates only to listed wetlands, whereas "wise use" applies to all wetlands. While the Convention does not define those terms, the Conference of the Parties (COP) currently defines "promote conservation" and "wise use" as, respectively, "maintenance of the ecological character" and "maintenance of their [wetlands] ecological character, achieved through the implementation of ecosystem approaches, within the context of sustainable development" (COP 2005, Resolution IX.1 Annex A, p. 6; COP 2008b, Resolution X.15, p. 3; COP 2015a, Ramsar Strategic Plan 2016–2024, p. 6). Thus, Contracting Parties are also required to maintain the ecological character of unlisted wetlands *as far as possible*. The "ecological character" is defined as "the combination of the ecosystem components, processes, and benefits/services that characterize the wetlands at a given point in time" (COP 2005, Resolution IX.1 Annex A, p. 5). An obligation to maintain accords with the object of the Convention "to stem the progressive encroachment on and loss of wetlands now and in the future" (Preamble:[4]), rather than a duty to restore them to some earlier preferred state.

According to the COP, however, the obligation to maintain, together with the reporting requirements of Article 3.2, entails a duty to restore any "adverse change" in the ecological character (Pittock et al. 2010; COP 2008c, Resolution X.16), which is defined as "the human-induced adverse alteration of any ecosystem component, process, and and/or ecosystem benefit/service" (COP 2005, Resolution IX.1 Annex A, p. 6). According to the Strategic Plan 1997–2002, "[t]he aim is at least to maintain the ecological character recorded at the time of designation, and, in many cases, additional measures will be required to restore functions, values or attributes lost prior to designation" (Ramsar Strategic Plan 1997–2002, p. 13). The duty to restore pre-listing adverse change may practically be limited if there were a lack of pre-listing baseline ecological knowledge to assess the change (COP 2008b, Resolution X.15). This practical limit may be more prevalent for unlisted wetlands.

Does the duty to restore wetlands include a duty to restore environmental flows? The COP has recognized for many years that to maintain the ecological character of a wetland, "it is necessary to allocate water as closely as possible to the natural regime" (COP 2002a, Resolution VIII.1, p. 6). In 1999, the COP found that "[n]ational planning and legislation on protection and sustainable use of nature, environment, and water management should be developed to include obligations or, at least, options for wetland restoration" (COP 1999, Resolution VII.17, p. 4). In 2002, COP8 recommended a review of "water policy and legislation in order to establish clearly the legal status and priority of water allocations for wetland ecosystems in relation to water allocations for other uses" (COP 2002a, Resolution VIII.1, p. 9). COP8 also recognized "that large dams ... affect wetland hydrology" and "that a significant proportion of globally threatened and non-threatened species ... are highly vulnerable to the direct and indirect impacts of dams" (COP 2002b, Resolution VIII.2, p. 1). Parties were urged to pay particular attention to wetland restoration in catchment and river basin management in relation to water allocation and management to maintain the ecological functions of wetlands (COP 2002, Resolution VIII.16). COP8 resolved that "[a]dequate water has to be provided to wetlands to sustain the functioning of ecosystems ..." (COP 2002a, Resolution VIII.1, p. 6; see also COP 2015b, Resolution XII.12).

In June 2015, continuing wetlands degradation led COP12 to call for action on the water requirements of wetlands in adopting the Ramsar Strategic Plan 2016–2024 (COP 2015b, Resolution XII.12). The Plan vision is that "[w]etlands are conserved, wisely used, *restored*, and their benefits are recognized and valued by all" and the Plan's second target is that "'[w]ater use respects wetland ecosystem needs ...'" (Ramsar Strategic Plan 2016–2024, p. 6 and 13). The Plan is the basis for implementing the Convention and says the Parties "should" implement it (i.e. the Plan) at national and regional levels (Ramsar Strategic Plan 2016–2024, p. 10). We conclude that there is a duty to allocate environmental water when necessary to maintain the ecological character of the wetland, including restoring adequate water flows.

There are, however, several challenges to implementing this duty. First, apart from the ecological character, restoration requires knowledge about the water requirements of each particular wetland (COP 2015b, Resolution XII.12). Already in 2002, Parties were urged to "undertake the systematic implementation of environmental flow assessments, where appropriate, to mitigate socio-economic and ecological impacts of large dams on wetlands" (COP 2002b, Resolution VIII.2, p. 2). If such knowledge is not available, then the precautionary principle should be applied (COP 2002a, Resolution VIII. 1; COP 2015b, Resolution XII.12).

Secondly, the Convention framework does not provide guidance on how to distinguish human-induced change from "naturally occurring change" (COP 2008d, DOC. 27). The distinction becomes particularly complex in the context of climate change (COP 2008d, DOC. 27). For example: "[W]hile excessive water diversions are clearly human induced [...], water diversions that have historically been considered acceptable may become excessive with the impacts of climate change" (Pittock et al. 2010, p. 422). Can such impacts of anthropogenic climate change be classified as "human-induced adverse change" to the wetlands under the Convention obligations? Pittock et al. (2010) argue that they are in relation to the Murray Darling Basin. While the Convention framework does not clearly connect the two, it observes that the "increase in global average temperatures since the mid-twentieth century is very likely due to the increase in anthropogenic greenhouse gas concentrations" and recognizes "that global climate change is likely to exacerbate the loss and degradation of many wetlands" (COP 2008e, Resolution X.24, p. 3). Similarly, Australian Government agencies recognize that "it is extremely likely that the dominant cause of recent warming is human-induced greenhouse gas emissions and not natural climate variability" (BoM and CSIRO 2014 p. 10). We conclude that there is a duty of restoration in response to climate change.

Thirdly, the duty to restore is subject to certain qualifications, including physical possibility (Pittock et al. 2010; COP 2008c, Resolution X.16). Even where it is possible to restore, the Party may decline to do so because of "urgent national interests" (COP 2008c, Resolution X.16), which are determined solely by the Party (COP 2002c, Resolution VIII.20, p. 3). Public drinking water supply and irrigation of food fall within this term. These qualifications present domestic political challenges to implementing the international duty to restore, including the analysis of the legal status of the duty.

Another argument associates a duty to restore wetlands with the Ramsar Convention. There is an increasing association between the Ramsar Convention and the Convention on Biological Diversity (CBD), which contains explicit obligations for *in situ* and *ex situ* restoration (Articles 8(f) & 9(c)). The Ramsar Strategic Plan 2016–2024 emphasizes the lead role of the Ramsar Convention in the implementation of wetland activities under the CBD (CBD 1996, Decision III/21). This may strengthen the Ramsar duty to restore wetlands with biodiversity values.

In summary, the Ramsar Convention COP resolutions and Strategic Plan establish an international duty to restore the ecological character of wetlands by provision of environmental water flows. The COP also proposes that this duty be legislated domestically. In Australia, international obligations only take effect in domestic law when the Commonwealth or a State legislates to implement them.

EPBC Act 1999 (Cth)

The *EPBC Act* includes three main mechanisms for implementing the Ramsar Convention obligations for listed wetlands: (1) designation of wetlands for listing, (2) environmental assessment and approval of "actions" that may adversely impact on them, and (3) the preparation and implementation of plans for their conservation in co-operation with the States and Territories (Gardner 2012). The third of these is the most relevant to restoring human-induced adverse change to wetlands (*EPBC Act* Sections 328–336). For wetlands in a State:

"The Commonwealth *must use its best endeavours to ensure a plan* for managing the [listed] wetland in a way that is not inconsistent with Australia's obligations under the Ramsar Convention or the Australian Ramsar management principles is *prepared and implemented in co-operation with the State* or Territory." [emphasis added] (EPBCA Section 333(2)).

This qualified duty to cooperate with the States is elaborated in the *Environment Protection and Biodiversity Conservation Regulations 2000* (Cth), Regulation 10.02 and Schedule 6, which prescribe the Australian Ramsar management principles. They provide that each declared Ramsar wetland "should" have "[a]t least 1 management plan" that "should" (Clause 2.01–2.02):

- Describe the ecological character of the wetland and what "must" be done to maintain this character;
- "state mechanisms to deal with the impacts of actions that individually or cumulatively endanger its ecological character, including risks arising from" changes to water regimes;
- state whether restoration or rehabilitation is needed and, if so, explain how the plan provides for this.

There is no guidance on how to respond to climate change.

In summary, the *EPBC Act* provides a qualified duty of cooperation to make and implement a management plan rather than a duty to restore. The Commonwealth need only uses its "best endeavours," a term which appears to have no recent judicial interpretation in application to Commonwealth action. Commonwealth-State agreement is required to fulfill this duty.

The content of a plan should accord with the management principles as subordinate legislation. The Commonwealth must not contravene or authorize contravention of a plan (Section 330), but the *EPBC Act* gives a plan no greater legal force against a State than it would have as an agreement with the Commonwealth, enforceable only by themselves. The Commonwealth may induce agreement by financial assistance (*EPBC Act*, Section 336).

The RIWI Act and EP Act of WA

The legal duties to make EWAs under these two Acts were considered in detail in 2006 and the position remains unchanged (Gardner 2006). The *RIWI Act* provides for governmental authorization of taking water resources. The *EP Act* provides discretionary authority to make legally binding environmental protection policies and give environmental impact assessment approvals. The two Acts neither address the Ramsar duties to maintain or restore the ecological character of wetlands nor give any guidance on responding to a drying climate.

Conclusion

In conclusion, there is not an unqualified legislated legal duty to restore waterways and wetlands by ensuring adequate water flow, neither internationally nor nationally. However, the Ramsar Convention framework creates international obligations to restore listed wetlands at least to the ecological character of their time of listing and to maintain the ecological character of all other wetlands as far as possible. These duties include providing adequate water to sustain wetlands as functioning ecosystems, including in response to adverse effects of climate change. While physical possibility and urgent national interests are acknowledging qualifications to these duties, the CBD duty to restore wetland biodiversity values may strengthen the core duties. These obligations help establish political expectations and define the scope of domestic authority to legislate for restoration.

The WA water resources reform should impose water planning duties on the Minister for Water to:

- identify and publish within a defined time (e.g., 1 year) the EWAs needed to maintain and restore the ecological character of all Ramsar listed wetlands, taking account of the water that would naturally, i.e. considering the impact of climate change but before consumptive use be available to sustain that ecological character;
- approve plans for those listed wetlands within 4 years (an electoral cycle) to establish EWAs that allocate water as closely as possible to the natural regime, as affected by climate change, within 10 years or the term of the plan, if less; and
- use best endeavours to make plans to establish EWAs that maintain the ecological character of all unlisted wetlands as far as possible, especially those that have high biodiversity values.

The Commonwealth should amend the *EPBC Act* to require the national Minister to certify publicly and report to the COP that the State plans comply with the Ramsar obligations and, if they do not, to exercise a step in power to make the EWAs within 3 years (an electoral cycle).

There will be great social and economic factors to contend with in fulfilling these duties. Water scarcity for a growing population in a drying climate is a multidimensional problem requiring investment in social and technological change to manage demand and develop alternative water sources. The suggested duties are ultimately procedural but mandate restoration decisions.

Acknowledgments

The authors acknowledge Commonwealth funding received from the Co-operative Research Centre for Water Sensitive Cities to undertake research contributing to this article and the valuable insights gained by Alex Gardner participating in the "Restoration Dialogues" symposium held at the University of Tasmania, Australia, in November 2015.

References

Agriculture and Resource Management Council of Australia and New Zealand and the Australian and New Zealand Environment and Conservation Council (ARMCANZ and ANZECC) 1996, 'National Principles for the Provision of Water For Ecosystems'.

Bennett, M and Gardner, A 2014, 'How do environmental conservation laws interact with environmental aspects of water laws?', *Environmental and Planning Law Journal*, vol. 31, pp. 3–10.

Bureau of Meteorology, Australian Government (BoM) and Commonwealth Scientific and Industrial Research Organisation (CSIRO) 2014, 'State of the Climate'.

Comino, MP 1997, 'The Ramsar Convention in Australia – improving the implementation framework', Environmental and Planning Law Journal, vol. 14, pp. 89–101.

Conference of the Parties to the Convention on Biological Diversity (CBD) 1996, 'Wetlands and biological diversity: cooperation between the Convention on Wetlands of International Importance Especially as Waterfowl Habitat (Ramsar, Iran, 1971) and the Convention on Biological Diversity', Decision III/21. Argentina.

Conference of the Parties to the Convention on Wetlands (COP) 1996, 'Strategic Plan 1997–2002, adopted at the 6th Meeting of the Conference of the Contracting Parties'. Australia.

COP 1999, 'Restoration as an element of national planning for wetland conservation and wise use', Resolution VII.17. Costa Rica.

COP 2002a, 'Guidelines for the allocation and management of water for maintaining the ecological functions of wetlands', Resolution VIII.1. Spain.

COP 2002b, 'The Report of the World Commission on Dams (WCD) and its relevance to the Ramsar Convention', Resolution VIII.2. Spain.

COP 2002c, 'General guidance for interpreting "urgent national interests" under Article 2.5 of the Convention and considering compensation under Article 4.2', Resolution VIII.20. Spain.

COP 2005, 'A Conceptual Framework for the wise use of wetlands and the maintenance of their ecological character', Resolution IX.1 Annex A. Uganda.

COP 2008a, 'The Ramsar Strategic Plan 2009–2015', Resolution X.1, adjusted by Resolution XI.3 (2012). Republic of Korea.

COP 2008b, 'Describing the ecological character of wetlands, and data needs and formats for core inventory: harmonized scientific and technical guidance', Resolution X.15. Republic of Korea.

COP 2008c, 'A Framework for processes of detecting, reporting and responding to change in wetland ecological character', Resolution X.16. Republic of Korea.
COP 2008d, 'Background and rationale to the Framework for processes of detecting, reporting and responding to change in wetland ecological character', DOC. 27. Republic of Korea.

COP 2008e, 'Climate change and wetlands', Resolution X.24. Republic of Korea.

COP 2015a, 'The Ramsar Strategic Plan 2016–2024', Resolution XII.2. Uruguay.

COP 2015b, 'Call to action to ensure and protect the water requirements of wetlands for the present and the future', Resolution XII.12. Uruguay.

Convention on Wetlands of International Importance especially as Waterfowl Habitat (Ramsar Convention) 1971', 'Australian Treaty Series No. 48'.

Department of Water (DoW) 2012, 'Assessment of ecological health and environmental water provisions in the Harvey River', Report no. 44. Western Australian Government.
DoW 2015a, 'Western Australian Government Water reform, Legislation'. Available from: <http://water.wa.gov.au/legislation/water>. [12 February 2016].

DoW 2015b, 'Personal Communication from Drew B on 2 November 2015'.
Environmental Protection Act 1986 (WA).

Environment Protection and Biodiversity Conservation Act 1999 (Cth).

Gardner, A 2006, 'Environmental Water Allocations in Australia', *Environmental and Planning Law Journal*, vol. 23, pp. 208–235.

Gardner, A 2012, 'The legal protection of Ramsar Wetlands: Australian reforms' in *Environmental Governance and Sustainability*, ed P Martin et al., Edward Elgar, Cheltenham, UK, pp. 193–217.

Kingsford, RT 2000, 'Ecological impacts of dams, water diversions and river management on floodplain wetlands in Australia', *Austral Ecology*, vol. 25, pp. 109–127.

National Water Commission 2004, 'Intergovernmental Agreement on a National Water Initiative'. Available from: <http://www.nwc.gov.au/nwi>. [12 February 2016].

Peel-Harvey Catchment Council and others (PHCC) 2009, 'Peel-Yalgorup System Ramsar Site Management Plan', Western Australian Government.

Pittock, J, Finlayson, M, Gardner, A and McKay, C 2010, 'Changing character: the Ramsar convention on wetlands and climate change in the Murray–Darling basin. Australia', *Environmental and Planning Law Journal* 27, pp. 401–425.

Rights in Water and Irrigation Act 1914 (WA).

APPENDIX Releases (ML) from North Dandalup Dam

Year	Monthly total												Total	Percentage of inflow (%)
	Jul	Aug	Sep	Oct	Nov	Dec	Jan	Feb	Mar	Apr	May	Jun		
2006–2007	67.5	28.4	–	14.0	51.9	53.5	89.7	84.3	91.5	89.8	94.2	83.6	784.4	11.5
2007–2008	71.5	20.4	–	–	21.4	69.4	59.8	68.3	72.9	64.7	9.9	–	458.3	3.6
2008–2009	–	–	2.6	22.1	51.0	52.7	79.2	90.6	81.8	75.0	82.8	84.1	621.9	7.4
2009–2010	87.8	3.3	–	16.9	32.8	50.6	87.1	77.2	84.8	84.2	87.4	55.1	667.2	3.9
2010–2011	48.5	39.1	37.6	36.1	36.2	48.7	63.2	53.3	69.2	60.5	54.8	1.9	549.1	126.4
2011–2012	–	–	–	–	16.5	42.9	70.4	86.3	77.6	74.8	10.3	–	378.8	3.6
2012–2013	–	–	–	–	12.2	22.6	64.3	41.3	51.2	45.9	24.1	–	261.6	3.5
2013–2014	–	–	–	–	35.1	75.1	80.7	67.5	78.4	70.3	57.6	–	464.7	5.5
2014–2015	–	–	–	–	12.6	50.1	78.1	84.2	85.0	74.5	27.5	–	412.0	2.9
2015–2016	–	–	–	23.0	30.0	46.5	69.8	63.0	69.8	60.0	31.0	–	393.0	43.7
Average	27.5	9.1	4.0	11.2	30.0	51.2	74.2	71.6	76.2	70.0	48.0	22.5	499.1	21.2
Average monthly total 2006–2016:													41.6	
Average yearly total 2011–2016:													382.0	
Average monthly total 2011–2016:													31.8	

The numbers entered for releases over the 2015–2016 Summer are estimated using similar dry year releases from the Summers 2010–2011 and 2012–2013.

Information kindly provided by DoW (2015b).

New Water Policy and Practice - Volume 2, Number 2 - Spring 2016

The Riverfront as a Mirror: The Case of the Transformations in Post-Soviet Cities

Jorge Gonçalves,[A] Davit Asanidze[B] and Pedro Pinto[A]

Cities that have gone through the long period of integration in the ex-Soviet Union naturally incorporated a set of principles that are now under pressure. It's in this context that we review the central question of the relationship between river and city.

Tbilisi, Georgia, is representative of the challenges faced by cities that experienced the fast transition from state-controlled to open-market economies. Territorial planning, as a single system of state spatial planning, is presently still highly unstructured and has very little practical influence, with several urban planning decisions being made with little regard for formal urban planning agencies. One of the key issues in the capital city, Tbilisi, is the lack of green/recreational zones, which is also expressed in the loss of public space along the urban riverfront.

Undermanaged growth of post-Soviet city, expiration of the term of the last general plan, and disregard for historical traditions of city planning resulted in an abnormal and complex problem of interplay between Tbilisi and River Kura. The river has been, in the last few decades, striped of its architectural planning significance.

Interrelation between Tbilisi city and the River Kura constitutes a complex and challenging urban problem but their transformation is related also with political aims. Kura, as an essential active element of the landscape, is being used to influence the city's planning character and as political instrument.

This presentation highlights, through an overview of some relevant examples from Tbilisi of planning and design, how the interface zones between river and surrounding plots of land have been transformed to increase urban–river connectivity. Yet, this transformation also results in the emergence of urban projects that symbolize more political and economic powers that the aspiration of the people to appropriate public spaces.

Keywords: Urban space, riverfront, urban rehabilitation, post-Soviet city, Tbilisi.

[A] Cesur-CEris, IST-UL, Portugal

[B] IST-UL, Georgia

doi: 10.18278/nwpp.2.2.4

1. Introduction

Water has been a central element to urban development throughout most of urban history (Mann 1973). Today, there is a most-welcome rediscovery of the role of urban rivers as central elements in urban qualification, especially noticeable in public spaces interventions (Busquets 1997; Mann 1988). However, for various reasons, that was not always the case, especially during the Industrial Era. The detachment between cities and their rivers was pervasive, namely in Western and Eastern European cities.

In the case of Tbilisi, Georgia, and especially since the last century, the different moments registered in the relationship with the Kura River are the results of shifting cultural values that, at each time period, were assigned to the river or even public open spaces. Traditionally, the expansion of Tbilisi was generally concentrated along the valley and hills bordering the Kura River, and its banks occupied a central location in the city's urban structure. More recently, though, urban development has shifted away to more distant sectors, far removed from the river, taking advantage of the best opportunities for the real-estate business. (Salukvadze & Golubchikov 2016).

The river has been understood as a valuable economic asset throughout most of history. The availability of water could attract many industries and the river served as a major trade and communication route.

When this interest waned by the emergence of alternative locative factors, the Soviet administration took this opportunity to launch large road infrastructure skirting the river in order to support the rapid urban growth that occurred during this period (Salukvadze & Golubchikov 2016). Both urban sprawl and the creation of these large barriers formed by linear infrastructure were symptomatic of the growing distancing between the city and its river. To a city whose identity was so intrinsically interwoven with the Kura, this was nothing short of an identity reconstruction, which all-but-eliminated one of the most fundamental elements of the city's urban identity. The post-Soviet period of Tbilisi, while convoluted, has coincided with a slow recovery of this damaged relationship between city and river.

The complex and rapidly shifting socio-economic context over which recent project have been taking place is reflective of the contradictions and limitations inherent to a complex and on-going process of construction of a democratic society and an open economy system.

The specificities of Soviet planning and diversity of post-Soviet transformations and experiences is rightly emphasized in the critical literature on the studies of Eastern European and former Soviet societies under transition (Hann 2002; Tsenkova 2014). Following the collapse of state socialism, central and eastern European cities went through a period of deep changes, in a process of fast and uneasy adaptation to very different rules and mechanisms. The legacy of socialism can be considered as a main aspect of the structure of post-Soviet cities (Tsenkova 2014). Changes in the national stages of transformation were different and influenced by not only the post-Soviet heritage, but also by contemporary drivers. The current forces also contribute to establish new processes (Grazuleviciute-Vileniske & Urbonas 2014). We will focus on the example of Georgia and its capital city, Tbilisi.

The greatest changes started after the collapse of the Soviet Union. The state-controlled economy of former Soviet Republics transitioned quickly to free market policies after their independence and under new political leadership, Georgia being among them (Asabashvili 2011). This context is very different from that of Western Europe, and therefore demands a specific approach, diverse from that used when analysing recent trends in western urbanization. According to Sykora and Bouzarovski (2012), the main topic of argument is that the process of more fundamental restriction of urban morphology of the central and eastern European cities is still ongoing, while the transformation of main economic and political principles is formally over.

The peculiar zoning and spatial segregation and hierarchy patterns deriving from Soviet-era urbanism are still present (Darieva, Kaschuba & Krebs 2011). Due to character (for instance, the virtual absence of private land/initiative in city development), the Soviet planning system was not applicable to the new reality, during a tumultuous transition to independence and free market, where there were no alternative strategic or spatial plans being created. Old Soviet regulations were formally expanded, but given their inadequacy, they were extremely inefficient in the new reality (Tsenkova 2014).

As the government mechanism, focused mostly in the building of housing, failed, the leading role was taken by the construction businesses, which were emerging quickly and took full advantage of the situation: no control system, prosperous corruption, and crime in the country, all of which gave raise to uncontrolled developments in the town centers. This period was sadly characterized by massive constructions in public parks, squares, and public land with disregard for any basic norms of planning, design, or construction applied. Today in Georgia, the legacy of the 1990s is still visible, especially in Tbilisi. The development policy based on the neoliberal market has just become formalized. Therefore, anyone who can pay a fee can build above the height and volume limits, even if theoretically against the standing planning rules (Asabashvili 2011).

The riverfront plays a key role in the process of urban development. Given its connection to the river and intricacy, the riverfront steers the space production on the river's edges. They are centrally located and available for reshaping. Post-Soviet riverfront areas are undergoing rapid transformation. All this is happening under demanding conditions: the political system and administrative structure is still rebuilding, with the economy suffering large pressures to change, and a real-estate market that seems gradually exposed to large financial interests but is yet devoid of effective control by planning institutions and legal/ technical standards. It is under this framework that we should interpret the changes to post-Soviet urban riverfronts.

According to these aspects the riverfronts became conflict areas (Machala 2014). Waterfronts are usually used as pro-growth strategies in the developing cities or hold symbolic value regarding the city planning or the city marketing (Short et al. 1993).

2. Fundamentals of Urban Development of Tbilisi Riverfront

At all stages of Tbilisi's development, the braided, multi-channel course of Kura River, was a pervasive influence. In the past, the river was vested with navigation functions also. Apparently, the downgrade of watercourse level throughout the periods was largely caused by the depletion of forest stands alongside its embankments. The River Kura area, as a linear image of Tbilisi composition, also plays an important role in the sense of city extension, and has a direct effect on microclimate. The masses of air passing alongside the Kura gorge have a potential for ventilation of the capital. Nowadays, large and small islands between river banks have vanished and the river confined to a single channel, while on the 1800 map even gardens of such islands are depicted (Kvirkvelia 1985). The 1800 map (see Figure 1) is the first "modern" and accurately drafted map of the city, and is therefore fundamental in understanding past urban processes. This map provides graphical images of densely inhabited districts, the street network, particularly of buildings and parts of the city ruined by the last invasion of Agha Mahmood Khan in 1795, which makes it trustworthy source to rely on when studying Tbilisi city planning in late eighteenth century (Beridze 1991).

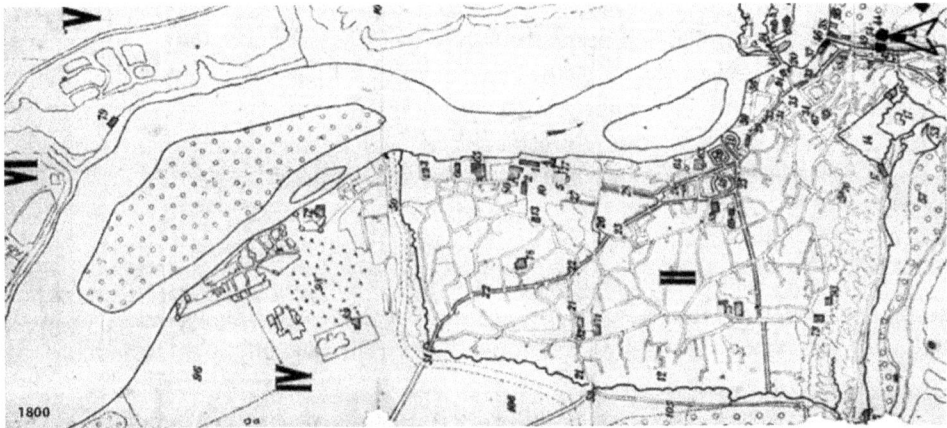

Figure 1. 1800 Plan of Tbilisi, Georgia. Source: National Parliamentary Library of Georgia

In the late feudal age, Kura defined the unique structure of not only of the riverside, but, due to the diminutive scale of Tbilisi, also the structure of the entire city:

- The core living sector was laid down the meadow and thus all key administrative, commercial, sports, and entertaining establishments and places of worship were situated alongside the river bank.
- The Embankment was perceived as a prestigious part of the city, for the reason that representatives of nobility and upper social class erected their palaces and premises exactly on this spot.

• Tbilisi is typified with humid climate and the river bank was favorable space for aeration (Pochkhua 1999).

The river powered four mills across the banks. Different types of factories, such as breweries, grape, and fruit beverage plants, lather and soap productions, were actively operating together with tobacco, textile, lumber, and brick plants (Suny 2009). Whilst arranging recreational zones, the utmost and decisive importance has always been attached to the factor of river. This was a rather complex process, but at all stages the Kura served as an axis with amusement and leisure places all flanking it.

Following the political alterations in the early nineteenth century, a new administrative center was established further inland, in the "Garetubani" and thus detached from Kura River. This caused loss of some positive impacts (such as, hygienic importance of the river and its effect on environment), to which the royal center had been adjacent until the late feudal age (Pochkhua 1999).

After repositioning Tbilisi administrative center away from the Kura neighborhood, all major buildings were constructed along the new Rustaveli Avenue. However, the ancient cultural monuments, which retained their importance and indeed deserved growing appreciation, as icons of the city's rich architectural heritage and spacious installations of the historical surrounding, still remained in the old town, alongside Kura, where the stream of the river together with its tributaries was the definitive structuring element of the centuries-old city structure. This fact itself demanded special reconstruction programs, which was unfortunately not taken into consideration by professionals (Pochkhua 1999).

In studying and analyzing the 1923–1934 first general city plan of Tbilisi, first and foremost we ought to take into account the role of Kharkov's "GIPROGRAD" institute for planning, which without a doubt had effect on the entire planning structure of the city and its image, as well as on the future fate of Kura and its banks. Regrettably, the project not only prescribed the relocation of most of the city's core functions to a new location, down the river, which was historically common for Tbilisi's planning, but it also refrained from conducting a proper analysis and research of the nature and purpose of the river, its composition, and development perspectives (Pochkhua 1999). Practical works, aimed at reinforcing river banks for subsequent construction of highways, commenced in 1928 (Janberidze 1979). In the second half of 1930s, Soviet Authorities demolished watermills (Kardava 2013) and after lowering of river level, embankments were secured and the Rike district was constructed over a reclaimed plot of land (Kvirkvelia 1985).

During the Soviet era, industrialization and city expansion were very active (Salukvadze & Duineveld 2009). That is the reason that the city has the structure of linear development, which could be seen as the source of many of today's transportation problems along the Kura river valley (Gachechiladze 1995). The works for elevation of Kura banks were launched in 1947. The left embankment was occupied by a new transportation highway, after the erection of load-bearing wall was finalized in 1948–1949. The restructuring of the embankment was followed by the reconstruction of the surrounding area. Marshes along the right tributary of the Kura were desiccated, and afterwards converted into a new park, where river meadows and old cabins once stood, on the former Orbeliani Island. The embankment followed the trail of the former dry stream-bed under the bridge (Janberidze 1979).

An issue of "The Communist" newspaper, dated January 21, 1951, proclaimed that: "Many things have been changed. Previously a backward part of the city nowadays shines with various novelties. There are no more watermills erected along the banks of Kura with large wheels. Instead, now the load-bearing wall follows the river and soon the new, beautiful embankment highway will be completed, stretching between the reconstructed bridges of Baratashvili and Marx." However, the first secretary of central committee, Kandid Charkviani, who was among those who orchestrated reconstruction of Kura banks, claimed that pulling down the watermills had nothing to do with the construction of banks and new bridges. Reshaping of Kura embankment and erection of river dams made it impossible to assemble watermills over Kura (Kardava 2013). The construction of embankment highways in the 1940s was greeted as a major improvement to the sanitary conditions of the city of Tbilisi, but at once fostered an estrangement process between the Kura and many Tbilisi neighborhoods. Those highways to some extent relieved traffic in long streets on both sides of Kura, but the problem of transportation still remained unresolved (Pochkhua 1999).

As a consequence of the construction of main roads dictated by necessity, it's impossible not to bypass the deterioration of the aesthetic potential of the historic central districts of Tbilisi, as and the Kura riverbanks, a consequence of all these major works. This phenomenon may be observed through the lens of comparative analysis among pre and post-construction photo materials (see Figure 2).

Figure 2. (Left and right) River Kura Embankments, Soviet Period. Tbilisi, Georgia
Source: *National Parliamentary Library of Georgia*

Construction of embankments continued in Tbilisi. If in 1940 total length of the armored banks amounted to 3 km, in 1966 this length was increased up to 13.5 km. Kura was channelized and straightened through the city and its banks were transformed into the major highways. River banks replaced Central Avenue's role as the main transport axis and played a key role in connecting Navtlugh to Saburtalo via freeway (Janberidze 1979).

Setting out the embankments, paradoxically, triggered a revival of the old trend in the development of Tbilisi, namely properly linking city parts to the Kura banks and amplifying the importance of river zone itself as a central area. The tunnel dug further north in the bedrock served the purpose of preserving settlements over Metekhi hill and beyond as well as continuation of high-speed freeway alongside the left embankment.

Throughout the 1940s–1950s, the old tradition to set recreational zones, such as parks, along the river banks had been mostly lost. At the same time, utilization of river waters for technical rationales fostered the tendency to orient industrial zones around the river basin, which had a critical effect on aesthetical image of banks and on the ecology of the river. Considering the long-term trend, it becomes evident that pollution of Kura and its tributaries kept increasing and subsequently water quality was severely degraded within the area of Tbilisi. This process is unfortunately ongoing, having persisted to this day despite the fact that overall produce and industry is lessened. Sewage and wastewaters still remain the main source of pollution of Kura basin (Gventsadze 2013).

3. Recent Riverside Interventions

3.1 Project of the Rike Riverside Park

Rike, which lies along the left bank of the River Kura, is situated between Avlabari and Chugureti districts (see Figure 3). In the middle ages, Rika was the name given to the entire left bank area of Kura, but later this name was substituted by Chugureti. In the seventeenth century, the Rike area served as a competition field for wrestling and for other sport activities. The Avchala road, leading to Russia, started from here. In the nineteenth century, city fairs and markets were arranged here. As Rike is located in the lowest level of the city, on the Kura embankment, the area was usually severely affected by flooding (Kvirkvelia 1985).

In 2009, Tbilisi City Hall took up work on the idea of rehabilitation and development of the city's historical part. The program united several large-scale projects, among them and foremost the renovation of Rike Park. The Park space is divided into three main areas with the following objectives:

- Restoring balance between residential and recreational areas inside the historical center of the city;
- Filling the deficiency in greenery of the city;
- Enhancing living convenience for historical densely districts over the river;
- Transforming Tbilisi center into important portion of the city; and
- Creating opportunity for genuine link to the river.

The project of the 7.5 hectare park was approved by the Tbilisi City Hall in 2010 without any prior public discussions (see Figure 4). The project's author is a Spanish architect, Domingo Cabo. The City Hall did not disclose information on details of construction. Among other issues, interested urban specialists were not given the chance to access the data on expenditures. The main shaping element of the Rike Park is a 3D moving fountain, which serves as a connection along the main pedestrian circuit from "Bridge of Peace" toward the promenades assembled over the roof of a new segment of the Avlabari tunnel. The "tunnel," running above the ground along the banks but under a ledge which provides an extension for the public space, is used as an element of the park and is well integrated into the entire space. It should nevertheless be noted that the pedestrian zone is restricted to a strip between the river and the new segment of the tunnel, while all remaining areas are overwhelmingly being used as a parking lot.

Figure 3. Location of Rike Riverside Park. Tbilisi, Georgia

Figure 4. Rike Riverside Park. Tbilisi, Georgia

Here, the "Buda Bar" was opened alongside the promenades. As is the case with franchises from this brand, the "Bar" is required to be enclosed from the surrounding area, further decreasing the provision of actual public spaces within such a large area. Consequently, the area behind the Bar remains cut-off from the river bank. Therefore, this part of the park could not retain the functions of reconnecting the city and the river that were supposedly at the project's heart, and the "Bar" now acts to artificially split the river with the rest of the Park area. A person walking through the riverside promenade, basically located on the ledge over the tunnel, is blocked landwards by an ungainly wall preventing connections inland.

The cleverly designed parking lot for 350 vehicles is constructed under the Park. However, during evening and night rush hours the space is half-empty, despite the fact that Gorgasali circus (<150 m away) is tremendously overwhelmed by cars parked at the surface. Presumably, this is caused by ineffective management.

The new bridge and the Rike Theatre constitute one single unit, but due to their scale and aesthetics are awkwardly out of context with the surroundings (see Figure 5). Despite the smart location of the bridge, it appears overbearing given the volume of glass, and the bridge produces an extremely conspicuous visual obstruction affecting the viewshed along Kura's gorge. This lack of concern for the context in symbolic architecture should definitely be addressed in future interventions. Rike Theatre is particularly hard to perceive for a person walking down the Baratashvili Bridge toward the Park, because the construction is almost fully hidden from sideway view from the inner part of the Park, as if it had been designed to be exclusively viewed from across the river and not by those walking by it.

Figure 5. New Bridge and Theatre in Rike Park. Tbilisi, Georgia

Construction of the new riverside park doubtless grants overwhelming approval by everyone in the city; however, the project itself caused huge controversy among society, because the connections to the Kura and its landscape deserved very little concern in the project for this recreational zone. The territory was freed from the old ugly restaurants, which was a positive for sure, but the new buildings erected thorough the Park (bridge, theatre, tunnel, and cable car station) are absolutely off the context of this historical district.

Therefore, criticism should be raised toward the options and process surrounding the design and selection of these new structures, currently dominating the area. Here, major landscaping-shaping elements are Metekhi temple, Narikala fortress, Sioni Cathedral, and a segment of old Tbilisi settlements, which are harmoniously merged with the River Kura and its banks and form the unique territory of Rike. All previous authorities were cautious when making concrete decisions in relation to these areas of the city. Numerous contests had been arranged together with public discussions, and winners were announced more than once. However, Rike still remained preserved before the implementation of this Project. Within the city center, this was the only available area which allowed for a frank improvement of the connectivity between the city and the river but, nowadays, this is virtually impossible given the options taken in planning of the new Rike Park and its oversized and ill-fitting constructions (see Figure 6).

Figure 6. Bridge of Peace, Rike Park. Tbilisi, Georgia

3.2. Deda-Ena Garden Project

The greening of the Deda-Ena Garden (former Orbeliani Island) started in 1930s, during the simultaneous construction of the Kura embankments. The area, previously utilized for agricultural and industrial purposes, was transformed into the recreational zone (Janberidze 1979). Unfortunately, this green area (total 9 hectare) has been progressively reduced with the construction of new buildings, during the last 15 years (see Figure 7).

Figure 7. Location of Deda-Ena Garden. Tbilisi, Georgia

The new Public Service Hall (the building of which sacrificed a formerly very popular tennis court complex) was successfully added to this territory. The Tennis Courts were of emblematic, often being compared to the "Wimbledon" of Tbilisi, and currently the Service Hall complex occupies a total of 5 hectares, 2.5 of which is allocated for parking (see Figure 8).

The project aimed at constructing an iconic public building in the city center along the riverside, which would attach new and interesting shades to the surrounding environment, comparable to the effect of the Guggenheim Museum of Bilbao.

The project for the Public Service Hall was a continuation of the Rike Park project. The project by Italian architect Massimiliano Fuksas was unilaterally approved without preceding tenders or public discussions. The total area of the seven floor building is 2.7 hectares, and it includes offices and service spaces. It holds a complex program in a sensitive and historically significant area, which makes it somewhat baffling that the architect didn't deem it necessary to visit the place and study in situ the impact factors of the space. The river performs an important role in shaping the city and, naturally, development of riverfront infrastructure affects the riverside landscape, determining dramatically the city's image.

Figure 8. Comparison of Changes between Soviet Time and Nowadays. Tbilisi, Georgia
Source: National Parliamentary Library of Georgia

Pedestrian paths alongside the Kura embankments define the planning structure of the territories surrounding river. During the Soviet period, these sidewalks were much wider and assigned the role of boulevard and riverside promenade; even today the city lamps can be seen along the river embankments.

Embankment roads were not so overloaded with traffic in earlier decades and thus pedestrian access across them to the riverside promenade was much easier. In 2012, after completion of the construction of Public Service Hall, the cars toll dramatically raised around the area and, with the purpose of widening the roadway, authorities cut off the trees alongside the bank and tapered the pedestrian pavements. Moreover, during the construction process, a large number of trees were additionally cut off for the building site as well as for establishing surface car parking. Such actions give the impression of a general indifference towards nature and the environment (see Figure 9).

Figure 9. New Parking Lot Front of the River Kura. Tbilisi, Georgia

However, those responsible for transforming the city's landscape declared that the entire process was well planned and there was no reason to point out the devastating consequences of it as such aftermath was "likely unexpected." This negligent approach has resulted in loss of dozens of trees. Even more damaging, the image of city's old park, its functionality, and connection to its adjacent neighborhood has also been sacrificed.

As with the Rike project, once again, a disproportionate amount of the surface space is devoted to car parking, when formerly it included large areas of public space. Given the size and cost of the project, it would not have been difficult to consider the opportunity to create underground parking so as to increase the provision of riverfront public promenades, all-too-rare in central Tbilisi. Given the project's extremely large budget, adding this element would likely have a minimal impact over the total costs and would have permitted the off-set of some of the worst negative impacts of the project.

4. Conclusions

As we have observed, changes in the post-Soviet cities are supported by huge economic and political transformations. However, this process is still in flux, as a result of a yet incomplete switch from entirely different systems of land-use planning and, indeed, land ownership. Democratization and regulation processes have been slowly incorporated, but have not been able to keep pace with much-faster trends in development, which are still vastly controlled by private developers and, sometimes, with the complicity of a seemingly unwitting public administration. This leads to a half-baked incorporation of some core values of Western societies, in which some staples, such as environmental protection or public participation, have not been transferred or properly taken into account. As Van Assche, Verschraegen, and Salukvadze (2010) refer the ongoing democratization process has not allowed the development of urban management tools to defend fundamental values such as public involvement or environmental qualification resulting in urban interventions that do not include all the interests involved.

These transformations of the riverfront, being emblematic projects of a new political, economic, and financial power, end up being used as over-priced symbols, with their merits being weighed almost exclusively based on the visual appeal as isolate units, far outweighing rather the consideration of more structural problems of the Kura's riverfront that indeed direly require attention, such as the provision of riverfront public spaces or reestablishing connection between neighborhoods and across the banks.

The two projects along the banks of the Kura are emblematic of the structural problems that still need to be addressed in the planning structures and institutions. In order to further prevent such insensible decisions and events, as those triggered by these projects, first and foremost one should address what is the purpose and objective of the territory alongside river banks; only after understanding, and adequately balancing, competing land uses, should the projects develop into the design stages, in order to avoid the casuistic and often insensible way "iconic" buildings have been dictating all other space arrangements in recent projects, as well as compromising the image of this area of Tbilisi.

The urban transformations taking place along the river's banks are very enlightening as to the type of development that these cities are suffering. They occur in a context where political and economic powers are not sufficiently supervised by an intense public participation. The planning authorities are yet to fully adapt to the new socio-political reality and are therefore still recovering their role as supervisors and leaders in the design and improvement of public spaces. While this was more or less a given while all land transformation initiative was public led, the new context of strong private initiative requires further enforcement of the public's role as a mediator and a supervisor of planning and design standards.

There is a good reason to believe, based on our analysis, that the collective interest is not always safeguarded in these recent riverfront interventions, namely in terms of the types of land uses being pushed forward or the provision of public open spaces. We recognize the great importance and the qualifying role that the Kura River and its banks provide to the city of Tbilisi. Nevertheless, while riverfront interventions have certainly contributed to once again highlighting this role, the solutions adopted fail to optimize the potential benefits to the city. While the scenic power of the river has been explored as a way to promote the visibility of a few buildings and landscape elements, the actual benefits to the residents and workers of the neighboring areas are limited. This is a consequence of the inappropriate mix of uses and lack of public open areas, but also of a much insufficient articulation of these spaces with pre-existing street patterns. The result is that these spaces remain somewhat detached from everyday circulation patterns for Tbilisi's residents and works, when they should be encouraging the rediscovery of the river's banks as a central space within Tbilisi.

Going beyond the simplistic reading of the river as a mere framing element of urban "qualification," we consider that the river Kura could have a much greater role in city life, still possible through a new set of interventions along its banks. These would have to take into account elements that, for the greater part, were absent from the recent projects: they should promote the use of the river and its banks for the transport of persons and goods, instilling it with vibrancy, emphasizing its economic importance, and promoting alternative, cleaner, modes of transport; the environmental quality of the river itself should be the object of a basin-wide management plan, identifying and supporting the elimination of multiple sources of pollution. The improvement of the water quality should encourage more daring urban interventions promoting the proximity between people and the River. These developments will likely only be possible once local, regional, and national planning agencies are equipped with stronger mandates and the technical and political capacities to lead the planning process. Henceforth, they should be able to determine the design and implementation of riverfront interventions and enforce solutions that best suit the collective interest of the city and its citizens.

References

Asabashvili, L 2011, *Lived Transitions*. Available from: <http://urbanreactor.org>. [29 April 2015].

Beridze, G 1991, 'Gegmarebiti Tradiciebi XIX Saukunis Tbilisis KalaktmSheneblobashi', *Kartuli khelovneba*, pp. 89-101.

Busquets, J 1997, 'Los Waterfront de nuevo una prioridad urbanística', *Mediterrâneo*, vol. 10(11), pp. 35-46.

Darieva, T, Kaschuba, W & Krebs, M 2011, *Urban Spaces After Socialism: Ethnographies of Public Places in Eurasian Cities*, Campus Verlag, Frankfurt/Main.

Gachechiladze, R 1995, *The New Georgia: Space, Society, Politics*, UCL Press, London.

Grazuleviciute-Vileniske, I & Urbonas, V 2014, 'Urban Regeneration in the Context of Post-Soviet Transformation: Lithuanian Experience', *Journal of Cultural Heritage*, vol. 15, no. 6, pp. 637–643.

Gventsadze, N 2013, *Tbilisis Istoriulad Chamokalibebuli Natsilis Hidrokselis Kalakmaformirebeli Roli*. PhD Thesis, Georgian Technical Univesity, Tbilisi.

Hann, C 2002, *Postsocialism: Ideals, Ideologies and Practices in Eurasia*, Routledge, London.

Janberidze, N 1979, *Kartuli Sabchota Arkitektura*, Khelovneba, Tbilisi.

Kardava, D 2013, *Mtkvari da Misi Ori Napiri*, Bakur Sulakauri, Tbilisi.

Kvirkvelia, T 1985, *Arkhitektura Tbilisi*, Stroyizdat, Moscow.

Machala, B 2014, 'The Uneven Struggle for Bluefields: Waterfront Transformation in Post-Socialist Bratislava', *Hungarian Geographical Bulletin*, vol. 63, no. 3, pp. 335–352.

Mann, R 1973, *Rivers in the City*, Praeger Publishers, New York.

Mann, RB 1988, 'Ten Trends in the Continuing Renaissance of Urban Waterfronts', *Landscape and Urban Planning*, vol. 16, no. 1, pp. 177–199.

Pochkhua, M 1999, *The Link Between Town-Planning Structures and River Mtkvari in Late Feudal Tbilisi*. PhD Thesis, Georgian technical Univesity, Tbilisi.

Salukvadze, J & Duineveld, MA 2009, 'Would Planners be as Sweet any Other Name? Roles in a Transitional Planning System: Tbilisi, Georgia' in *City Culture and City Planning in Tbilisi: Where Europe and Asia Meet*, eds K Van Assche & J Salukvadze, Edwin Mellen Press, Lewiston, pp. 243–303.

Salukvadze, J & Golubchikov, O 2016, 'City as a geopolitics: Tbilisi, Georgia—A globalizing metropolis in a turbulent region', *Cities*, vol. 52, pp. 39–54.

Short, JR, Benton, LM, Luce, WB & Walton, J 1993, 'Reconstructing the Image of the Industrial City', *Annals of the Association of American Geographers*, vol. 83, no. 2, pp. 207–224.

Suny, R 2009, 'The Mother of Cities: Tbilisi/Tiflis in the Twilight of Empire' in *City Culture and City Planning in Tbilisi: Where Europe and Asia Meet*, eds K Van Assche & J Salukvadze, Edwin Mellen Press, Lewiston, pp. 17–55.

Sykora, L & Bouzarovski, S 2012, 'Multiple Transformations: Conceptualising the Post-Communist Urban Transition', *Urban Studies*, vol. 49, no. 1, pp. 43–60.

Tsenkova, S 2014, 'Planning Trajectories in Post-Socialist Cities: Patterns of Divergence and Change', *Urban Research & Practice*, vol. 7, no. 3, pp. 278–301.

Van Assche, K, Verschraegen, G & Salukvadze, J 2010, 'Changing Frames: Citizen and Expert Participation in Georgian Planning', *Planning, Practice & Research*, vol. 25, no. 3, pp. 377–395.

The Impact of Art in Social Movements to Protect Water in the Northern Rivers Region in NSW

José Javier Serrano[A]

This article is founded upon research that was inspired by the lovely community of the Northern Rivers Region and their passionate, artistic, and nonviolent way to protest against coal seam gas mining in the area. It was completed during the course of the Masters of Integrated Water Management which was instructed by the International Water Centre at the University of Queensland premises.

Residents of the NRR claim that CSG Industry may pollute shared water resources, destroy the land, and ruin the scenery for them and future generations. Having little political, legislative or National Government support, the community organized and educated themselves in order to create a national grassroots organization called "Lock the Gate Alliance" that fosters policy changes to stop CSG activities unless it is proven safe for the environment, natural water resources, land, and health.

The Alliance's activities follow principles of nonviolence and community participation, which have inspired creative and artistic ways to create awareness about current CSG processes, to educate people, to raise funds, and more. The inclusion of art expressions in the Alliance's social movements have encouraged resident participation, leading to increased social capital. As a result, the Alliance has progressed in the social movement lifecycle following a path to success.

***Keywords**: Northern Rivers Region, coal seam gas, fracking, social movements, nonviolent action, water*

Introduction

Water is essential for life. Its effective use and management is mandatory in order to face challenges such as population growth and food security (UNESCO 2006). Art is known for its ability to create an emotional link

[A] Universidad Regional Amazónica IKIAM—International Water Centre Alumni Network.

doi: 10.18278/nwpp.2.2.5

between a piece of art and its audience which has the potential to influence the viewer. This gives art the capacity to unite people by sharing the same emotions via visual and auditory communication. Communication through art entails any activity where a sender transmits experienced feelings by external signs (Tolstoy 2015). These two fields, water management and art, can be related since both involve social dimensions. An effective implementation of Integrated Water Resource Management (IWRM) depends on technical and scientific knowledge and collaboration between stakeholders (ICWE 1992) which often conflicts.

It is agreed that the management of water use is a concept well understood (Lenton & Muller 2009). In practice however, there are some gaps. This is mainly because the first steps of water and resource management are often determined by individual stakeholders who focus on their own particular interests. They sometimes do not consider or know that every individual action has unintended consequences—either positive and/or negative—for other stakeholders (Lenton & Muller 2009) and for the environment as a network of natural systems (Carey 2012).

In this article, an attempt is being made to address the following question: what is the impact of art in social movements that aims to protect water and land? This study aims to find the effect of art expressions used in the case study of Northern Rivers Region (NRR) social movements against coal seam gas (CSG) industry, in terms of purposes, effects on people, and in the dynamics of the social movement itself. All of this understanding is based upon local perspective and is related to IWRM principles.

First, a brief description about the case study, CSG extraction method (fracking), and legislation ruling CSG extraction in Australia will be explored. Next, community art concept, theory of social movements' dynamics, stages to successful nonviolent social movements and community art concepts will be presented. Finally a more detailed explanation of the art presence in social movement will be described along with conclusions on their impact on social movements to protect water.

Northern Rivers Region

The case study selected was the NRR which is located in the Australian state of New South Wales (NSW) constituted by major towns such as Byron Bay and Nimbin grouped in seven local government areas (Tweed, Kyogle, Byron, Lismore, Ballina, Richmond Valley, and Clarence Valley) (Anon 2012). It is one of the most biodiverse areas in Australia with a strong agricultural sector and organic production (Anon 2012). Permaculture practices are so common in this area that a Permaculture Research Institute (Permaculture Research Institute 2016) was founded, which is located in the Channon (part of Lismore area). Having strong agricultural practices, water is an essential resource for NRR's residents.

Coal Seam Gas in Australia

In Australia CSG has been an expanding industry since 1996 (Carey 2012). State Governments and CSG Industry promise users that CSG extraction technology does not contaminate water, damage the environment or negatively affect nearby populations, and it is also a profitable business (Santos 2012). CSG is a multi-billion dollar industry holding licenses granted by the Government for mining exploration and exploitation that covers large portions of Australia. Since 2003, CSG production has increased on average by 32% each year (Carey 2012). The extensive development of the industry, since 2008, has been difficult to monitor and has been mostly active in Queensland (QLD) and New South Wales (NSW).

The NRR residents, in NSW, have shown concern about this expanding industry because of water quality, environmental consequences, and health impacts. As a result, people have initiated social movements against the CSG industry adopting a nonviolent approach in an artistic way.

The NRR's residents showed a clear discontent against CSG industry by claiming that it will pollute the region's water resources, destroy land, and ruin scenery (Lock the Gate Alliance NR 2012). As a result, residents have been operating, since 2010, a national grassroots group called "Lock the Gate Alliance" that applies a nonviolent approach to achieve policy change (Lock the Gate Alliance 2015). Grassroots group organizations can be defined as "local political organizations that seek to influence conditions not related to the working situation of the participants and which have the activity of the participants as their primary resource" (Gundelach 1979).

CSG Extraction—Fracking

CSG is a natural gas trapped by groundwater and then pressurized in the pores of coal seams. Mainly methane is extracted from deposits which are located very deep underground. In order to get to the deposits, steel-cased wells are drilled into the coal seams to release the gas (Carey 2012). This method is used because it is very costly to dig using traditional mining procedures.

The process to drill into the coal seams is known as *hydraulic fracturing* or *"fracking."* CSG is extracted by drilling wells vertically until reaching gas rich stratum. Once there, horizontally drilling is performed to increase access to the gas. Water mixed with sand and chemicals is pumped under high pressure to accelerate the flow of the gas by fracturing the coal seams allowing the gas to flow to the surface through the well. To prevent cross-contamination, the wells are cased with cement and steel to separate the gas flow from the aquifers (Carey 2012).

There are many concerns in general about the hydraulic fracturing process (Carey 2012). The chemicals used to pump water into the wells are associated with contamination of water resources (Osborn et al. 2011) and potential tremors caused from drilling and water pumping (Weinhold 2012).

What does the Legislation say about CSG in Australia?

The NRR mining policies and regulations in regards to CSG are under NSW legislation. In NSW legislation, CSG is classified as petroleum. Under the Petroleum (onshore) Act 1991 (NSW) the ministers and departments responsible for CSG are as follows:

- The NSW Minister for Resource and Energy (responsible for the onshore petroleum, and granting leases and licenses).
- The NSW Department of Trade and Investment Division of Resources and Energy—Minerals and Petroleum.
- The NSW Minister for Planning and Infrastructure (grants development consent).
- The Planning Assessment Commission (assists the Minister for Planning to assess development applications, sometimes it can take the Minister for Planning and Infrastructure's place into the decision-making processes).
- Local councils (limited involvement).
- The Minister for the Environment (involved in some cases where CSG activities are related to National Parks or Protected Areas).

According to the Section 6 of the Petroleum (onshore) Act 1991 (NSW), the Government owns the petroleum (CSG) on and under a piece of land and has the power to authorize exploration and exploitation. The only exception is if the petroleum reserved to the landowner has been issued under an old title system (Petroleum Act 1991 NSW s.6), however, this is very rare. CSG exploration and exploitation is regulated by several acts.[1] Leases and licenses are granted to the gas companies to allow them to explore and extract CSG from the ground but they also need a Development Consent.

A Development Consent is the approval for activities classified as Designated Development. It is granted by the Minister for Planning and Infrastructure after being assessed by the Department of Planning and Infrastructure. Some activities do not require Development Consent, such as stratum studies (to obtain details of rock formations but not for mineral deposits) and monitoring wells (to obtain water samples and monitor underground water levels). Within the Environmental Planning and Assessment Regulation schedule 3, clause 4, part 1, title 27(g), Petroleum works

---

[1] Petroleum (Onshore) Act 1991 (NSW), Petroleum (Onshore) Regulation 2007 (NSW), Environment Protection and Biodiversity Conservation Act 1999 (Cth), Environment Protection and Biodiversity Conservation Regulations (Cth), Environmental Planning and Assessment Act 1979 (NSW), Environmental Planning and Assessment Regulation 2000 (NSW), State Environmental Planning Policy (State and Regional Development) 2011 (NSW), State Environmental Planning Policy (Mining, Petroleum Production and Extractive Industries) 2007 (NSW), Strategic Regional Land Use Policies, Aquifer Interference Policy, Well Integrity Code of Practice, and Fracture Stimulation Activities Code of Practice.

are considered as Designated Development, therefore, require a Development Consent if they are located within a drinking water catchment, on a floodplain, within 40 m of a water body, areas with high water table or permeable soils (Australasian Legal Information Institute 2000).

According to the Mining Act 1992 (NSW), section 31, cl. 2, CSG exploration activities cannot be undertaken within 200 m of a house, 50 m of a vineyard, orchard, garden, or any important structure[2] unless the landowner provides written consent to the gas companies. Once it is granted it cannot be withdrawn. Any conflicts related to limitations are addressed by the Land and Environmental Court.

Community Art

Community art is a collaborative artistic process that involves community members and professional artists showing public expression and producing collective experience (Guetzkow 2002). It provides communities ways to express themselves and allows artists to use their talent along with the community.

Community art has proven that art, by itself, has a positive impact on people in different ways such as improving academic performance and discipline (Remer 1990), invigorating neighborhoods and fostering economic success (Costello 1997), improving physical and mental health (Mallory-Hill et al. 2012), and providing mechanisms for the creation of social capital (Hutzel 2007). The more exposed and active the community participation is, the more impact it will cause. It will impact the community, as a group, and its individual members at the same time. The impacts of art can be described in terms of social, human, and cultural capital. Social capital can be understood as networks of social relations based on trust and reciprocity, resulting in a shared benefit (Stone & Hughes 2002). Human capital is the experience, creativity, personality, skills, and knowledge of people (Becker 1964) and cultural capital refers to any noneconomic-related social assets, such as intellect, level of education, and writing and speech skills (Lareau & Weininger 2003).

It is important to mention that there is an exchange between different types of art expressions and the benefits they may produce (Guetzkow 2002). For example, theatre often uses professional staff for their shows which attracts more local audience and visitors from outside the community, therefore, generating economic benefit (depending on the level of attendance). There is however little community involvement as performers due to the lack of acting skills. As a result, theatre will have less potential to build social capital and community cohesiveness. The latter does not mean that theatre is always like that. Theatre can be used to build social capital and enhance community pride and sense of effectiveness.

---

[2] Large buildings, reservoirs, dams, contour or graded banks, levee, soil conservation works, water disposal areas, or any important structure defined as valuable by the Minister for Resources and Energy.

In terms of social movements, different expressions of art have been used throughout history as a mechanism for social change. Songs in Civil Rights Movements in the 1960s, feminist groups poetry, and theatre performances on the streets of Seattle against the World Trade Organization are some examples of expressions of art included in social movements. They have enhanced community empowerment by captivating those who are on the sides of the movement and drawn them into it (Reed 2005).

Community art provides an inclusive environment where any member of a community can contribute into a common expression of solidarity or a common goal. If a social movement is open to art expressions, it might attract the attention of musicians, performers, singers, acrobats, or people who have talents of a similar nature, who share the movement's perspective, and would communicate it to others using art.

Social Movements and their Life Cycle

What is a social movement? Some authors (Christiansen 2009; Polletta & Jasper 2001; Staggenborg 2011) have agreed that social movements are concentrations of people who use their skills and abilities to get things done, however, this is a broad definition. There might be groups of people that do not fit into a social movement category. For example, a soccer team is a group of people who use their ability to win a game. This cannot be classified as a social movement because their actions are not a reflection of political, social, or environmental issues that requires action.

Table 1: Stages of social movement life cycle

Stage	Description
Emergence	Widespread discontent of the current situation. There is little to no organization; only a few key movement participants who are well informed about the current situation. They might be unhappy with it in terms of policy, environmental, and or social conditions.
Coalescence	The "popular stage" where discontent is no longer individual and uncoordinated. It starts to get more focused and collective. This is a result of more knowledge about the issue and who or what is responsible for the problem.
Bureaucratization	Higher levels of organization and collective strategies. At this stage social movements cannot rely just on rallies or key leaders to move toward their goals. There is some success in raising awareness about an issue important enough that a social movement organization (SMO) is likely to be created.
Decline	Decline is the last stage of the social movement's "life-cycle." It is also known as "institutionalization."

Therefore, social movements in this article will be defined as temporary public spaces that supply people with identities, ideas, and ideals to establish a new way of life (Eyerman & Jamison 1991). They are driven by two key features: discontent with the current situation and aspirations to improve it (Blumer 1969). Social movements' life cycle can be presented in four stages as given in Table 1 (Christiansen 2009).

In Table 1, the term "decline" does not, however, mean failure. Instead, there are five ways in which a social movement can decline: repression,[3] co-optation,[4] success,[5] failure,[6] or by establishment within mainstream.[7]

Principles and Stages of Successful Social Movements

Bill Moyer, an activist who has studied social movements carefully, describes seven principles for successful social movements (Moyer 1987): social movements are proven to be powerful; movements are at the center of society; the real issue is social justice versus vested interest; the grand strategy is to promote participatory democracy; social movements focus on winning over ordinary citizens, not power holders; success is a long-term process, not an event, and social movements must be nonviolent. These principles were defined by researching successful social movements throughout history. This lead to define stages for a successful (nonviolent) social movement (Moyer 1990) shown in Table 2.

"Lock the Gate" Alliance

In Australia, representatives from over 40 professional, community, and environmental organizations in Queensland, NSW, Southern Australia and Victoria have started to show concern about the ongoing rapid expansion of the CSG industry. Consequently, they convened in Broke, NSW, to discuss the challenges of unrestricted CSG extraction. In the meeting, common issues such as health and environmental impacts were identified in communities where CSG extraction was implemented and expanded (Lock the Gate Alliance 2015).

The Government's lack of consideration for the opinion of local communities in the licenses approval was also raised in the meetings. This is how "Lock the Gate Alliance" was launched on November 22, 2010 and incorporated in NSW on December

---

[3] When authorities or representatives use actions to control or destroy the social movement, often using violence or altering laws.

[4] When the social movement is highly dependent on a centralized authority or on appealing leaders who come to an agreement with movement target authorities more than with the social movement itself.

[5] Consequence of achieving the change pursued.

[6] Due to strategic or organisational flaws at the organizational level.

[7] Occurs when aims and ideas are assumed by political, environmental, and social systems.

Table 2: Stages of successful nonviolent social movements

Stage	Description
Normal times	There are circumstances that violate freedom, democracy, security, and justice. Power holders are in total control of these circumstances by policies and the public is completely oblivious to the situation.
Prove failure of normal institutions	Public "upset levels" are proportional to the level of awareness of the policies that violate social values. People will become even more upset when they feel betrayed by politicians.
Ripening conditions	This is considered the beginning of a social movement. It requires documentation of the problem and organizing teams with experts. The social movement may get stuck in this stage if there is not a participatory environment between the growing grassroots groups and the small opposition groups. If the opposition power remains centralized in social movement organizations, small groups' creativity might be diminished. Creativity is a "natural resource."
The "Take-off"	The issue gets spread through news, newspaper, and social media and is publicly recognized as a social problem due to all the publicity about it. A trigger event reveals the problem to the public. Trigger events can be an accident or premeditated acts by particular individuals, opponents, or governments.
Perception of failure	After the peak of a trigger event a sense of despair might appear. Activists lose their motivation and faith to succeed thinking that the current policies will remain the same. They perceive the power holders to be too strong to fight against and their efforts they put on the activities were in vain. There is however, a perspective change from accepted policies to sources of problem.
Majority public opinion	The social movement that has reached this stage transcend from dealing with short-term crisis to a long-term struggle with the power holders.
Achieving alternatives – Success	Success is not a single event, it is a long process. This is the moment to swap from opposite current policies to a choice of which alternatives to adopt. There is substantial public desire for a change and power holders find it more costly to keep old policies and practices.
Continuation	Previous stage of success is not the end of the fight. However, it is the foundation for continuing that fight and creating new beginnings.

8, 2010 with the mission to protect Australia's natural, environmental, cultural, and agricultural resources from unrestricted mining and to educate, inform, and empower all citizens to demand sustainable solutions to food and energy production (Lock the Gate Alliance 2015).

The Lock the Gate Alliance (LTGA) is a national grassroots organization that aims to protect Australia's water systems, agricultural land, wetlands, bush lands, wildlife, health, and aboriginal and cultural heritage. All activities involve the following principles (Lock the Gate Alliance 2015).

- Decision making is guided by robust scientific assessment, the precautionary principle, and the principle of intergenerational equity.
- Communities have the ultimate say, within the context of the previous principle.
- It will support any community who supports the Alliance's objectives.

To achieve its aims, the Alliance has two main policy objectives (Lock the Gate Alliance 2015):

- Stop CSG exploration and exploitation until the community is convinced through sufficient, autonomous, and robust assessment that mining activities will not incur significant damage to the environment including water resource, land, health, and cultural heritage.
- Allow only sustainable and controlled mining that offers protection, health, and resilience of the community, the land they live in and their cultural heritage.

The principles of the Alliance clearly aim for sustainability. They encourage concepts such as stakeholder participation (power holders and community), social equity, and environmental protection, without dismissing the idea of mining if it is proven safe. The Alliance provides an inclusive environment for all the people to participate.

The group has undertaken several activities in a nonviolent context to reach as many people as possible with information campaigns and to achieve policy changes fostering sustainability. Residents are already informed about the current situation and they have shown a clear discontent to the uncontrolled and unjustified licenses granting.[8]

What are the Activities of the "Lock the Gate" Alliance?

LTGA undertake rallies, marches, and camps to inform, educate, and encourage people to become activists against CSG activities. They also organize blockades to

---

[8] The coordinator of the Gasfield Free Community Strategy in the Northern Rivers said (Dunoon and District Gazette 2013): "Of 11,590 people who have responded to the community surveys, only 89 people said NO to going Gasfield free (1%) and only 3% of the people said UNSURE. At what point will the Government listen to the people?"

prevent mining operations that jeopardizes water resources by fracking in NRR using a nonviolent direct approach (NVDA). Volunteers agree to be locked-on mining companies' vehicles in order to delay their actions. It is important to understand the passion and the role that people who volunteer to be locked-on have. By blocking mining companies' vehicles they are most likely to be arrested after spending hours in a very uncomfortable situation. Efforts to protect them are the focus of all participants. The NVDA works under given roles proposing a "buddy" system, which means there is a set of roles with different responsibilities at blockades.[9] One of the roles is also referred to as the "Peacekeepers" which includes, generally performers. Their main responsibility is to keep protesters and police entertained.

LTGA organize free pre-blockade workshops where participants are informed about legal aspects as protestors and landowners, peacekeeper principles, difficult behavior on-site, and police liaison training. Afterward, the participants attend the blockade to perform their assigned roles on-site. Despite the roles assigned, the "buddy" system presents some flaws affecting the outcome. Public discontent plays a major role in "demonizing" police. Some protestors let their emotions overtake and verbally attack police creating tension and conflict between the police liaison, the police, and themselves.

There is no organized communication with the media that is present on the blockades (media liaison role is nonexistent) passing this responsibility to the protesters who are responsible to record and spread information to the community. The use of social media, however, has become a powerful way to inform the community. Information on social media is less likely to be manipulated than information on regular media (e.g., hiding rude police behavior from the public). There is no defined logistical management role, however protestors voluntarily provide food, water, and power generators.

Art in the Alliance's Activities

Social movements can be a source of tension and stress for participants. However, it does not have to be like that. Participants of LTGA have found a way to ease tension by attracting people under an artistic and nonviolent approach. The following activities have incorporated some art expression and have been performed on blockades or outside the protest sites.

---

[9] Central contact person, police liaison, media liaison, food team, on-site communication team, transport, logistical management, physical and mental wellbeing, and artists and musicians. Based on the *Intercontinental deluxe guide to blockading*. This guide, however, is not available online anymore.

Coal Seam Gas "The Musical"

Organized by some of the same people involved in Terania Creek's protest,[10] the first successful environmental protest in Australia (Give Trees a Chance: The Story of Terania Creek 1980), the musical was seen as a way to educate, inform, and strengthen social cohesiveness by encouraging people to participate in the musical regardless of their acting skills. Everyone was welcome to participate and contribute with their own creativity on how to present different CSG-related topics such as: landowner rights, power holders' perspective, and consequences. Musicians were encouraged to create anti-CSG songs and marketing campaigns were undertaken by anti-CSG advertisers (pers. comm. April 29, 2013). After intensive rehearsal, music and creativity were put together to present "CSG The Musical" from June 28 to 30, 2012 raising around AUD$33,000.

CSG Idol

An open call for artists was advertised inspired on a known reality show by the same organizers of the "CSG The Musical." "CSG Idol" provided an opportunity for the residents to express their feelings about CSG. The open call included: musicians, singers, songwriters, poets, fashion designers, circus, cabaret, burlesque performers, choirs, groups, and flower arrangers. This initiative had several purposes, such as to raise funding and community engagement. The show attracted around 500 people, including donors and participants.

Knitting Nannas against Gas

Creativeness can encourage small and more localized events and groups. The most popular across the area has been the "Knitting Nannas against Gas," a peaceful group of elderly women (not necessarily, though) who sit outside politician offices and simply knit. Their main goal is to gain the attention of politicians and residents to inform them about the current situation related to land and water destruction by CSG mining, while teaching how to knit. They have become memorable for "dressing up" politicians banners with their art. Who would dare to harm or use police force against a group like this?

Girls against Gas

Another interesting group has been a center of attention, more focused in women participants, Girls against Gas, a group of superheroes who attend events, and blockades to fight against mining companies. The group was born from a group of girls

---

[10] The eco-protest was fighting for stopping the logging of the rainforest surrounding Terania Creek in the 1970s. The residents were appalled when they discovered the true plans of the Forestry Commission about logging the rainforest to sell the timber and replace it with eucalyptus.

who attended the NVDA training. They realized there was a lack of media attention to anti-CSG events. Wanting to solve this issue but keeping it in a fun way, they became superheroes dressed in yellow and black attending events to attract people and media to blockade locations.

Blockade Performing

Blockade locations can become event venues for musical shows. Doubtful Creek was a front line in the struggle to stop CSG activities in February 2013 (Australian Regional Media 2013). A peaceful camp was forced out of the Eden Creek State Forest by the police on February 4. This did not stop Andrea Soler and the Wadeville Mob (a local group of musicians from Wadeville and Kyogle) to perform a show at the road outside the forest (Knights Rd.) on February 9 to let the gas company Metgasco know what the public opinion about drilling activities was, in the nicest possible way. Wadeville Mob covered the front line with their anti-CSG songs (Australian Regional Media 2013).

Fence of Toys

On-site art expressions are welcome to ease tension, especially for children, who often attend events and blockades with their parents. On the field visit to a blockade conducted on February 7, an interesting visual expression made by children was placed at the fence of the Doubtful Creek drilling site (located inside a National Park). At that time, the Government had decided to prohibit access to the park. So, families encouraged their kids to cover up the fences with their toys so they can share and play with while being in the blockade, making their time less boring and getting to know other children.

Draining Funding

Community art with enough creativity has the potential to be used as strategy. One of the organizers of "CSG Musical" and "CSG Idol" came up with an idea to drain economic support from mining companies. The context of the idea originated from the fact that the "Baby Boom"[11] affected Australia between 1946 and 1961 (Salt 2001). From 2011 onward, these people started to reach their retirement age creating a "Retired Boom" now. The strategy was to create songs to encourage them to withdraw their funding from superannuation[12] companies that invest in CSG activities.

---

[11] Periods marked by an increase in birth rate. Generally they occur after war periods. The "Baby Boom" referred in this report is the Post-World War II.

[12] It is a way to save money for retirement by contributions made by employers based on the employee's salary.

The Impact of Art Incorporated into the "Lock the Gate" Alliance's Activities

The activities previously described demonstrate art expressions used in LTGA activities that have been born from participants' creativity and not from the LTGA methods themselves. The Alliance only fosters NVDA and the participants have put their imagination to include art, which after all, enhances cheerful behavior which fits to the purpose of the Alliance as well.

A review of the outcomes of LTGA activities delivered the following roles.

- Change people's perception: Informing about the current situation with true facts on a scientific basis in a nonbiased way; not to plant a thought in people but to encourage them to make a decision on their own, either for or against.
- Attract participants: Some activities can target different audiences. A broad range of creative activities gives a bigger opportunity to attract different groups (i.e., elderly women with the "Knitting Nannas" or young women with "Girls against Gas").
- Raise funds: Economic benefits can be achieved by activities like theatre or musical shows. Music performers and professional artists are more likely to volunteer when they share the same value as the social movement.
- Strategic purposes: Whether to attract media, Government attention, or specific people. Art can be a significant tool to create strategies that supports the purpose of the movement[13] (i.e., the sudden banning of Terania Creek Forest's Commercial attracted National attention to the issue of uncontrolled logging).
- Ease tensions: Especially during on-site events, where the situation might be difficult, community art can be important to diminish stress and increase tolerance.
- Creating networks: Using internet and online social network services (such as, Facebook and Twitter) to communicate achievements, share information, expose points of view, and keep people updated.

An activity can have one or more of the roles described simultaneously. Most of the activities undertaken by LTGA have multiple roles making them effective as community art. Some activities have also been adapted to become community art. Guetzkow (2002) presents a definition of Community Art from the Ontario Arts Council which specifically excludes knitting groups as a community art activity. However, the "Knitting Nannas against Gas" have changed that statement. In the end, it does not matter what type of community art is used but how is it used to enhance social capital.

---

[13] The "Terania Creek" protest inspired a polemic 30 seconds commercial with the motto "Would you share a road with a logging truck?" The commercial was released only for Lismore Council territory at election time, which caused it to be banned from being broadcasted due to a conflict of interests. Consequently, this sudden removal attracted national attention.

Impacts on the Lock the Gate Alliance's Life Cycle as a Social Movement

The Alliance's influence has reached a large amount of people, creating a common vision of the problem. It has reached some political levels, more specifically, the Parliamentary Secretary for Trade on the North Coast, Justine Elliot, who decided to resign her position because she wanted to join the fight against CSG industry and her convictions conflicted with the trade sector. She was the only Minister Parliament of the National Party who was against CSG mining (Elliot 2013).

Referring to the life cycle of social movements as previously explained (Table 1), the LTGA movement is aiming to decline by an establishment within mainstream. There is also room, less likely, for declining by success if LTGA achieves policy changes. There is no chance for co-optation since key participants of the Alliance are passionate enough to not accept any position with the government or mining companies that supports CSG activities.

Lock the Gate Alliance and the Stages for a Successful Nonviolent Social Movement

LTGA activities along with community art have contributed to make the movement follow the stages of a successful nonviolent social movement described by Moyer (1990) (Table 2), placing LTGA at the sixth stage—Majority Public Opinion. It can be claimed that LTGA started to use community art at the third stage (Ripening conditions) where opposition groups have grown in numbers with more people using their creativity to undertake NVDA activities to educate, attract, and recruit people for the emergence of the movement.

Through the use of community art, residents felt a higher degree of success in regards to the anti-CSG activities performed (as a result, skipping the fifth stage – Perception of failure). Community art also created awareness of the problem and current situation in regards to legislation, power holders, people's rights, and the potential risks to water and land resources. This collective thinking is reflected in the results of surveys conducted in >60 communities within the NRR claiming that 96% of people (from 11,590) are against CSG activities (Dunoon and District Gazette 2013).

Conclusions

In order to manage mining properly, it is important to have a balance between power holders and people's interests, natural resource management, and the environment. The case study selected was the NRR, which has been a target for CSG, resulting in discontent among residents due to the increased number of environmental licenses granted to undertake CSG activities, and the lack of public consultation and caring for water resources.

The main goal of this research was to explore the implementation of art expressions in social movements to protect water and land from CSG industry. The research focuses on the impact that art expressions can have on people, as an individual and as a community, to conform to a nonviolent social movement to fight for a common goal.

There is a difference between "citizen control" and "manipulation" (Arnstein 1969). What makes the difference is the power held by a community or social power. Social power enables communities excluded from political and economic developments to be included in decision-making processes in order to be a part of the shared benefits. Despite a clear public discontent and proven environmental and health impacts that CSG extraction process incur, exploration and exploitation licenses have been granted that overlook the environmental impacts and instead focuses on economic benefits only. Without the support of any power holders, residents have relied on collective power to raise their demands and try to force their interests onto political agenda.

Residents of the NRR have undertaken community art activities, which are leading the LTGA social movement to a path to success.[14] They have not achieved policy changes yet, but they have reached a major accomplishment, engaging people onto the values and aims of the Alliance. Some flaws have been detected in the way they undertake NVDA protests, with on-site action sometimes not consistent with the engagement framework. The reason for this is that people's aggressive emotions toward CSG industry are being channeled toward the police. Aggressive behavior creates conflict and distorts the original principles of nonviolence. The NVDA approach LTGA uses should be reviewed to address hostile behavior on-site, and the changes should be incorporated into the framework.

This research demonstrates that community art helped to engage residents, including different groups, and enabled them to participate, thereby fostering equity among community, strengthening social bonds, and increasing social capital. It also helped, and keeps helping, LTGA to expand across the country.

Under the IWRM principles of integration, the more people involved, the more they can influence political levels to involve all stakeholders from different management levels into policy development and planning processes. Any development that interacts with water resources should be able to meet social needs and have economic benefits. If there are environmental consequences, they should be addressed under government policies, taking into account stakeholder and end user observations. This is done to find a balance between economic, social, environmental, and political dimensions in order to have a sustainable development project.

---

[14] As defined in the stages of successful nonviolent social movements (Table 2).

References

Anon. 2012, *NSW Government*. Available from: <https://www.nsw.gov.au/sites/default/files/regions/regional_action_plan-northern_rivers.pdf>. [03 March 2016].

Arnstein, SR 1969, A ladder of participation, JAIP, vol. 35, no. 4, pp. 216–224.

Australasian Legal Information Institute, 2000. *Environmental Planning and Assessment Regulation 2000. Available from*: <http://www.austlii.edu.au/cgi-bin/sinodisp/au/legis/nsw/consol_reg/epaar2000480/sch3.html> [10 April 2016].

Australian Regional Media 2013, 'No doubt, get thee to the creek', *Lismore Echo* 7 February.

Becker, G 1964, *Human Capital: a theoretical and empirical analysis, with special reference to education*, National Bureau of Economic Research, Columbia.

Blumer, HG 1969, *Principles of sociology*, 3rd edn, s.n., New York.

Carey, M 2012, *Coal seam gas: future bonanza or toxic legacy*. Available from: <http://dea.org.au/images/general/viewpoint_issue_8_CSG.pdf>. [02 April 2016].

Christiansen, J 2009, *The four stages of social movements*. Available from: <https://www.ebscohost.com/uploads/imported/thisTopic-dbTopic-1248.pdf>. [2 April 2016].

Costello, DJ 1997, *The economic and social impact of the arts on urban and community development*, University of Pittsburgh, Pittsburgh.

Dunoon and District Gazette 2013, 'Casino anti-gas protest continues', *Dunoon and District Gazette* January, p. 11.

Elliot, J 2013, *Justine Elliot has stepped aside as Parliamentary Secretary for Trade* [Interview] (3 February 2013).

Eyerman, R, & Jamison, A 1991, *Social movements: a cognitive approach*, University Park, Pennsylvania.

Give Trees a Chance: The Story of Terania Creek 1980, [Film] NSW: Gaia Films.

Guetzkow, J 2002, 'How the arts impact communities: An introduction to the literature on arts impact studies', in *Proceedings of the Taking the Measure of Culture Conference*, June, Princeton University, New Jersey.

Gundelach, P 1979, 'Grass roots organizations', *Acta Sociológica*, vol. 22, no. 2, pp. 187.

Hutzel, K 2007, 'Reconstructing a community, reclaiming a playground: a participatory action research study', *Studies in Art Education*, vol. 48, no. 3, pp. 299–315.

ICWE 1992, *The Dublin Statement*. Available from: <http://www.wmo.int/pages/prog/hwrp/documents/english/icwedece.html>. [5 March 2016].

Lareau, A & Weininger, EB 2003, 'Cultural capital in educational research: a critical assessment', *Theory and Society*, vol. 32, no. 5/6, pp. 567–606.

Lenton, R & Muller, M 2009, *Integrated water resources management in practice: better water management for development*. Earthscan, London.

Lock the Gate Alliance 2015, *Lock the Gate Alliance*. Available from: <http://www.lockthegate.org.au/about_us>. [6 April 2016].

Lock the Gate Alliance NR 2012, *Petition of Northern Rivers residents against CSG, tight sands and unconventional gas*. Available from: <http://csgfreenorthernrivers.org/sandbox/wp-content/uploads/2012/07/Petition_CSG_12May-2012.pdf>. [6 April 2016].

Mallory-Hill, S, Preiser, WF, Preiser, WP & Watson, CG 2012, *Enhancing building performance*, Wiley, s.l..

Mining Act 1992, NSW. s.l.:s.n.

Moyer, B 1987, *Doing democracy. the MAP model for organizing social movements*, New Society Publishers, Canada.

Moyer, B 1990, *The practical strategist: movement action plan (MAP) strategic theories for evaluating, planning, and conducting social movements*, Social Movement Empowerment, s.l.:.

Osborn, SG, Vengosh, A, Warner, NR & Jackson, RB 2011, 'Methane contamination of drinking water accompanying gas-well drilling and hydraulic fracturing', *Proceedings of the National Academy of Sciences of the United States of America*, vol. 108, no. 20, pp. 8172-8176.

Permaculture Research Institute 2016, *Permaculture Research Institute*. Available from: <http://permaculturenews.org/>. [10 March 2016].

Petroleum Act 1991, NSW. s.l.:s.n.

Polletta, F & Jasper, JM 2001, 'Collective identity and social movements', *Annual Reviews*, vol. 27, pp. 283-305.

Reed, TV 2005, *The art of protest: culture and activism from the civil rights movement to the streets of seattle*, University of Minnesota Press, Minnesota.
Remer, J 1990, *Changing schools through the arts: how to built on the power of an idea*, ACA Books, New York.

Salt, B 2001, *The big shift: welcome to the third Australian culture: the Bernard Salt Report*, Hardie Grant Books, s.l..

Santos 2012, *CSG and water supply.* Available from: <https://www.youtube.com/watch?v=S2vCt8w-_Qc>. [01 March 2016].

Staggenborg, S 2011, *Social movements*, Oxford University Press, s.l..

Stone, W & Hughes, J 2002, *Social capital: empirical meaning and measurement validity*, Australian Institute of Family Studies. Available from: < https://aifs.gov.au/sites/default/files/publication-documents/RP27.pdf>. [6 April 2016].

Tolstoy, L 2015, *¿Qué es el arte?*, CreateSpace Independent Publishing Platform, s.l..

UNESCO 2006, *Water: a shared responsibility. The United Nations World Water Development Report 2.* UNESCO, Paris.

Weinhold, B 2012, 'NATURAL RESOURCES. Energy development linked with earthquakes', *Environmental Health Perspectives*, vol. 120, no. 10, pp. A388–A388.

Centralized versus Decentralized Wastewater Systems— Potential of Water Reuse within a Transboundary Context[1]

Sara Boavida[A], Mafalda Pinto[A], Teresa Salvador[A], Monther Hind[B] and Susana Neto[C]

Water management in transboundary situations is a multidisciplinary subject. The main objective of this article is to provide a reflection on the impact of centralized versus decentralized wastewater systems, regarding the potential of water reuse within a transboundary context. The Occupied Palestinian Territories are the presented scenario.

The existent wastewater treatment plants are not enough to guarantee good environmental and public health conditions and there are serious operational and maintenance problems. Due to the geopolitical situation in the Occupied Palestinian Territories, decentralized systems have been extensively used throughout the whole West Bank but most of the systems are not functioning correctly.

Two case studies are analyzed: Ras 'Atiya is an example of a possible transboundary wastewater management system where the wastewater treatment is proposed to be at an Israeli wastewater treatment plant and Atouf is based on a decentralized on-site system at household level.

In transboundary situations water reuse becomes a sensitive issue. Whenever there is centralized transboundary wastewater treatment, there is a risk that one of the parties involved may lose rights of its treated water.

Keywords: *Sanitation, transboundary water management, Palestine, Oslo II, water reuse*

[1] The present article was written based on the Final Report under the exchange and research work done within the European funded TRANSBASIN Project (295271 FP7-PEOPLE-2011-IRSES) with partnership of Israel, Palestine, Jordan and Portugal. The objective of this program was to provide a scientific forum for the establishment of a common ground for these basins as case studies of conflict and cooperation in river basin management and to identify the principles and mechanisms that both promote and hinder cooperation. Lessons learned from this project can be applied to other transboundary river basins in Europe and throughout the world. The three first authors had the same level of participation in this work supervised by Eng. Hind and Dr. Neto.

[A] Fundação da Faculdade de Ciências da Universidade de Lisboa, Portugal

[B] Palestinian Wastewater Engineers Group (PWEG), Al-Bireh, Palestine

[C] CERIS Instituto Superior Técnico, Portugal

doi: 10.18278/nwpp.2.2.6

Introduction

Water is one of the most important natural resources and remains under an increasing pressure due to its scarcity combined with the growth of population, increasing of economic activities, and the improvement of standards of living. Water is an environmental resource that neither knows nor respects political boundaries. Transboundary water management demands political cooperation and when this fails, it can lead to tensions and the breach of peace in regions in which political relations are fragile. The Occupied Palestinian territory (OPT) is a good example of this situation (Zeitoun & Warner 2006).

Non-conventional water resources, including water reuse, are especially important in water scarce areas (Shuval 2007). Considering also the present debate between centralized and decentralized wastewater management and systems, a question arises: "Is the impact of centralized versus decentralized wastewater systems relevant, regarding the potential of water reuse, and within a transboundary context?"

This article is part of the TransBasin project, Work Package 4—Protecting Groundwater and Enhancing Food Security through Low Cost, Decentralized Rural Sanitation, and is based on the Final Report by Boavida, Pinto, Salvador, and supervised by Hind and Neto (Boavida et al. 2015).

General Context

Country Profile

The OPT consist of two geographical entities—the West Bank and Gaza Strip (Figure 1). According to the World Bank (2015), OPT is considered a lower middle income country.

In 2014, the estimated population of the OPT was of 4.61 million. About 2.83 million live in the West Bank, and the other 1.78 million live in Gaza Strip (PCBS 2015c). The population is characterized by young demographics, high literacy, and over 26% of unemployment rate. The population natural growth rate in the OPT is 2.9% and the average household size is of 5.6 persons (PCBS 2015c).

OPT has a Mediterranean climate characterized by long, hot, dry summers and short, cool, rainy winters, with extremes dependent on altitude and latitude. January is the coldest month with temperatures from 5°C to 10°C and August is the hottest month at 18°C to 38°C (Weinberger et al. 2012).

Geopolitical Situation

Palestine and Israel are two neighboring states that are recognized by the UN although neither is universally acknowledged (Charbonneau & Nichols 2012; Jewish Virtual Library 2015). Therefore, both territories still do not have totally defined borders and still haven't created diplomatic relations as to allow peaceful co-existence.

Figure 1: Map of Palestine (West Bank and Gaza Strip). Source: United Nations OPT.

The most recent agreement between the two parties, the Oslo Accord II (also called the Israeli-Palestinian Interim Agreement), was signed in 1995 on the West Bank and the Gaza Strip. This agreement was supposed to have a transitory nature of five years with a shift from the areas under Israeli control to gradually become under Palestinian control. Nevertheless, by the year 2000 the failure in achieving another agreement and the beginning of the Second Intifada[2] gave Oslo II a more permanent nature (U.S. Department of State n.d.).

Oslo II divided the West Bank into three different areas (Israeli Ministry of Foreign Affairs n.d.; Selby 2013):

- Area A: comprising Jenin, Nablus, Tulkarem, Qalqilya, Ramallah, Bethlehem, and parts of the city of Hebron. In this area, currently 18% of the West Bank, the Israeli Defense Forces (IDF) withdrew, with the Palestinian Authority having full responsibility for internal security and public order, as well as full responsibility for civil affairs;

---

[2] The Second Intifada, also known as the Al-Aqsa Intifada, was the second Palestinian uprising against Israel — a period of intensified Israeli-Palestinian violence. It started in September 2000, when Ariel Sharon made a visit to the Temple Mount.

- Area B: corresponds to 22% of the West Bank and includes Palestinian towns and villages containing 68% of the Palestinian population. The Palestinian Authority grants full civil authority, as in Area "A," maintaining public order with the IDF overriding security authority to safeguard its citizens and to combat terrorism;
- Area C: comprising the unpopulated areas of the West Bank (60%) including all Israeli settlements and areas of strategic importance to Israel. The latter has full responsibility for security and public order and the Palestinian Authority assuming civil responsibilities not related to territory, such as economics, health, education, etc. (Israeli Ministry of Foreign Affairs n.d.; Selby 2013).

Figure 2 shows the map of the Areas A, B, and C as stated in the Oslo II Accord. This agreement stipulated that parts of Area C should be transferred to the territorial jurisdiction of the Palestinian Authority (Israeli Ministry of Foreign Affairs n.d.) nevertheless this never happened.

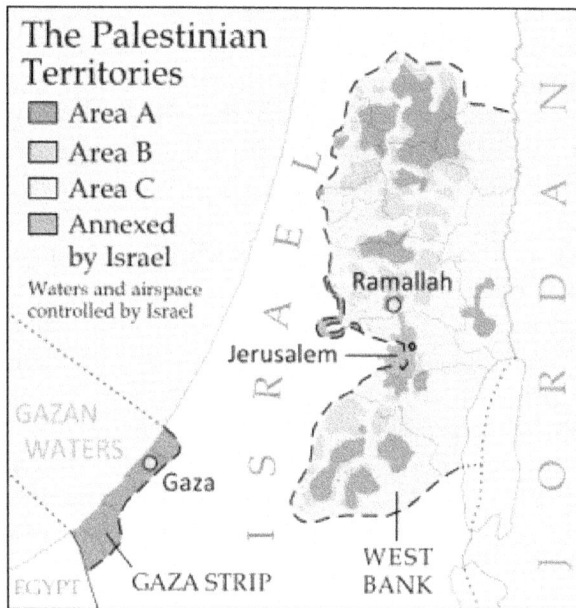

Figure 2: Map of the West Bank, Areas A and B. Source: The International Solidarity Movement (2014)

The fragmentation of the territory by the Oslo Agreement II resulted in the separation and encirclement of major Palestinian population centers by strategically located settlement blocs. Thus constraining the development of the Palestinian villages and populations and having a significant impact on approvals for water and wastewater projects.

Water Resources Governance

General Aspects

Israel, the OPT and other riparian countries partially share the water resources available in the region.

In 1995 the Oslo II accord established the basis for intended future negotiations and stated the principles of water and sewage management between Israel and Palestine.

The main source of water used for purposes such as drinking, agriculture, and industry comes from the existing aquifers. According to Weinberger et al. (2012), these resources have recorded a continuous fall in their annual recharge rates and most of these basins suffer from saline intrusion. Surface waters are concentrated in the northern and central parts of OPT and Israel and their drainage goes in three main directions: the Mediterranean Sea, Jordan Valley, and the Dead Sea. Besides the River Jordan and the Lake of Tiberias, it is estimated that there exist more than 30 major drainage areas generating circa 400 million cubic meters (mcm) per year.

Figure 3 illustrates the position and extension of all water resources existing in this region, together with the current borders of the West Bank and the Gaza Strip.

Within Annex II of Oslo II, *Protocol Concerning Civil Affairs*, the areas of agriculture, environmental protection, forests, nature reserves, parks, and water and sewage are addressed.

Article 40 is specific for water and sewage. The main principles address developing additional water resources, coordinating management of water resources and wastewater systems, treating effluent for eventual reuse, and ensuring water quality and the prevention of environmental damages. The creation of a Joint Water Committee (JWC) was proposed to support cooperation in the management and monitoring of water resources, water, and sewage systems. JWC is also responsible for the resolution of water and sewage disputes. According to Oslo II, this committee should comprise an equal number of representatives from both sides and all decisions have to be reached by consensus, which means that neither side has a veto.

Additionally, the division of the OPT into Areas A, B, and C created a great separation of the Palestinian territory. This did not allow continuity in the management regarding water issues, creating a barrier to the development of centralized policy and management for water and wastewater systems. For Palestinians the supply lines are localized, noncontiguous, and restricted Palestinian areas (A and B), the West Bank, and there is no means to import water or conveying water supplies between different regions of the territory (Selby 2013).

This article includes the estimation of the Palestinian water needs of 70–80 mcm per year for the supposed interim period, until year 2000. By this time Israel was committed to providing a total of 9.5 mcm of water per year to major Palestinian cities, including Gaza. The Palestinians were to be responsible for providing these areas with the additional supply of 19.1 mcm per year, of which 17 mcm should be drawn from

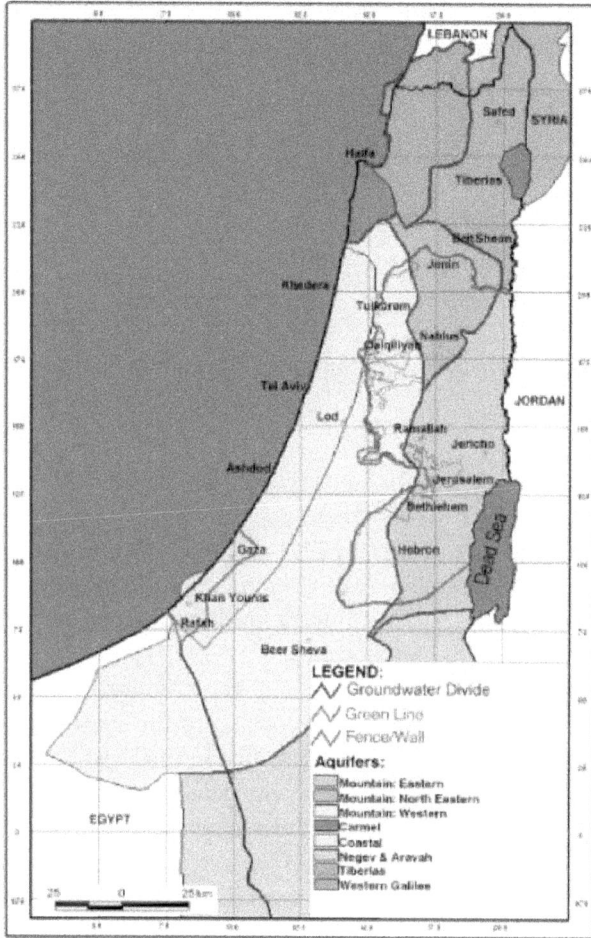

Figure 3: Transboundary Israeli–Palestinian water resources. Source: Amnesty International (2009).

the Eastern Aquifer. The remainder of the estimated water needs (41.4 to 51.4 mcm) was to be produced from the Eastern Aquifer, by Palestinians in accordance to the JWC.

The precise allowances for extractions and use of water from the Eastern, North-Eastern, and Western Aquifers are also stated in the accord, in Schedule 10 (Israel & PLO 1995). The rest of the water resources existent in the region, including river Jordan, are excluded from Oslo II, denying Palestinian access to them.

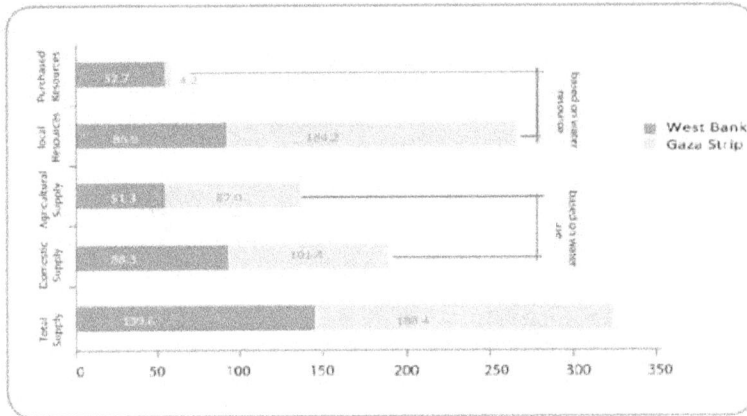

Figure 4: Selected Indicators for Water Supply in the Palestinian Territory. Source: PWA (2012).

Water Use and Abstraction in the Occupied Palestinian Territories

According to the PWA (2012), in 2011 the total of water supplied for domestic and agricultural use in the West Bank was 139.6 mcm, while in Gaza it was 183.7 mcm. From these volumes, 88.3 and 97.7 mcm were for domestic use for the West Bank and Gaza, respectively, as shown in Figure 4.

However, these figures do not represent the amount of water that is actually consumed in either of the OPT areas, as according to the same source, the losses on the domestic distribution water network reach 30% in the West Bank and 44% in Gaza (PWA 2012), respectively. In fact, more recent data concerning Gaza (PWA 2015) suggest that the efficiency of this system is even lower, with 58.9% of losses.

Thus, when considering the volumes of water abstraction only for domestic use in both the West Bank and Gaza, it is clear that the agreed amounts (or volumes) in the Oslo II are not enough to supply the current domestic and agricultural uses.

When taking into account the current population, these values translate to 79.3 liters per capita per day (l/c/d) in Gaza and 60.3 l/c/d in the West Bank. This level of water access is considered as intermediate by the World Health Organization (WHO) (Howard & Bartram 2003) and is below what is considered optimal access: 100 l/c/d. Only with the optimal access level is it possible to ensure very low risks of health concern. Additionally, according to the same source, intermittent water supply, as occurs in the OPT (Abu-Madi & Trifunovic 2013), implies higher health risks.

Presently, the West Bank would need at least 103.3 mcm per year just for domestic consumption to meet the WHO definition.

There are many reasons for the system's poor performance. Firstly, the old and leaky infrastructure, together with low water distribution tariffs do not generate enough financial resources for maintenance and contribute to OPT's dependence on foreign aid. Secondly, according to Oslo II, the system's operation and maintenance has to be done with consensus within the JWC, which, as stated by Selby (2013), may not be a straightforward process.

The current practices for water management pose a serious threat to the quality of the existing water resources.

Without taking into consideration future population growth or climate changes impact on water resources, it is already clear that future policies should aim to supply the entire population with the optimum access to water. Additionally, if taking into account water needs for economic development, 120 l/c/d is required (Chenoweth 2008).

Wastewater Generation in the Occupied Palestinian Territories

Once water is used it requires treatment and proper disposal methods to prevent environmental and public health issues. As a rule of thumb, circa 80% of the consumed water turns into wastewater and for OPT, most of it is lost on the surrounding environment. Although wastewater is usually seen exclusively as waste, once treated its reutilization may help diminish some of Palestinian water needs, especially for agriculture.

According to PWA (2012), it is estimated that in 2011 approximately 62.5 mcm of wastewater was generated in the West Bank. Currently, 35 mcm of untreated wastewater is discharged into the environment without any prior treatment (PWA 2015).

It is expected that the amount of generated wastewater will increase and environmental damages and public health threats related to poor wastewater management will also become more pressing issues. Shuval (2007) suggests that by 2025 this unconventional source of water will be essential to meet the water needs in the OPT.

Water Use, Abstraction, and Wastewater Generation in Israeli settlements

There is no official information about the Israeli withdrawal of water in the West Bank. According to an estimate presented by Shuval (2007), approximately 50 to 75 mcm per year are abstracted from the Mountain Aquifer, but there is no way to confirm the accuracy of these numbers.

According to Shreim (2012), there are 173 Israeli settlements in the West Bank, with 483,000 settlers. The same author suggests that each settler consumes approximately 343 litres per day, resulting the generation of about 60 mcm/year of wastewater. PWA (2012) presents a lower volume of 35 mcm/year discharged by settlements and industrial zones into the West Bank environment.

Some settlements have wastewater treatment plants (WWTP), with 31% of the wastewater being treated, but, the wastewater treatment is often inefficient and most of the times inexistent, leading to the discharge of this wastewater in wadis (streams) and fields in the West Bank (Shreim 2012). This constitutes a big threat to the shallow and deeper aquifers in the West Bank.

There are other cases, such as the P'sagot and Kohav Yaqob settlements near Ramallah, where the generated wastewater is treated at Al Bireh WWTP. According to the WWTP personnel, this connection was not predicted during the WWTP design.

Sanitation System Options

Centralized Systems and Decentralized Systems

Centralized systems are the most common type of sanitation systems. These systems include a wastewater collection and conveyance piping network, mechanical accessories and WWTP. They provide various levels of treatment that fit the desired final destination for treated water, but always present a trade-off between land availability and energy consumption (Bdour, Hamdi, & Tarawneh 2009).

In the OPT, one of the main concerns regarding the construction of centralized wastewater systems is land ownership and sovereignty. Wastewater decentralization is usually used whenever one or more of the necessary conditions for centralized systems do not exist. These systems are managed at the household or neighborhood level and usually use treatment options that require little or no energy consumption. They are generally implemented outside urban centers, typically in rural and agricultural areas (Tilley et al. 2014). Figure 5 presents a schematic example of the two systems.

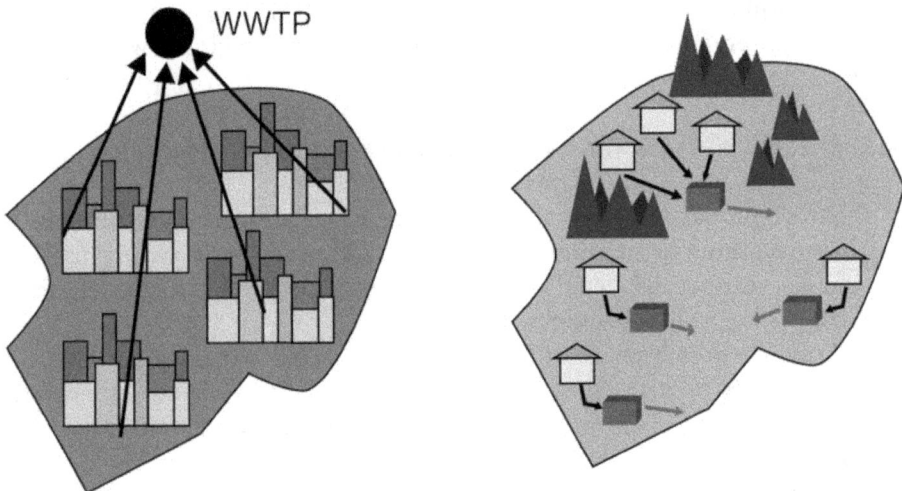

Figure 5: Scheme of Centralized and Decentralized Wastewater Systems.

Sanitation Service Levels and System Options

General Aspects

The wastewater sector in the West Bank and Gaza is characterized by poor sanitation services, insufficient treatment of wastewater, unsafe disposal of untreated, or partially treated water, and the use of untreated wastewater to irrigate edible crops (World Bank 2004).

The estimated percentage of the West Bank population connected to sewer networks in 2009 was 34.6% (Almasri & McNeill 2009) while the latest reports (data from 2014) indicate a rise to 45.3% of the national population (PCBS 2015c). The remaining population relies on cesspits to collect its wastewater (PCBS 2015c).

Centralized Treatment

Currently there are few fully operational WWTP in the West Bank. Table 1 shows the existing WWTPs in this region.

Table 1: West Bank WWTP Capacities

WWTP	Capacity
Nablus	30,000 m³/day
Ramallah	1,000 m³/day
Jericho	Up to 40,000 people equivalent
Taybeh and Ramoun	500 m³/day

There are two other WWTPs, in Tulkarm and Jenin, which were built in the mid-1970s with primary treatment only, and one in Ramallah that uses extended aeration technology. The Ramallah WWTP is currently beyond capacity and has not had any kind of extensive maintenance or intervention in the last four decades (PWA 2012).

Transboundary Treatment

Part of the untreated wastewater generated in the West Bank is discharged into *wadis* and flows to Israeli territory. According to PWA (2012) 15 mcm are treated yearly in Israeli facilities, most of which are located outside the 1949 Armistice Line.[3] Putting this into perspective, the treated water flow that becomes available to be used by Israel (15 mcm) is greater than the treated water Israel provides to the Gaza strip (10 mcm).

---

[3] 1949 Armistice Line: refers to the demarcation lines set out in the 1949 Armistice Agreements between the armies of Israel and those of its neighbors (Egypt, Jordan, Lebanon, and Syria) after the 1948 Arab–Israeli War, thus reaching an official cessation of hostilities of the first Arab–Israeli war that had started in May 1948 (https://en.wikipedia.org/wiki/Green_Line_(Israel)). The 1949 Armistice Lines between Israel and its Arab neighbors came to be known as The Green Line.

Treatment costs are directly deducted monthly by the Israeli government from the Palestinian Authority who loses the ownership over the treated water. Until 2011, the following WWTPs preformed treatment of transboundary waters (PWA 2012):

- Nir Eliyahu WWTP—treating wastewater from Qalqiliya. Presently this facility is known as South Sharon regional council WWTP (Yarqon River Authority 2015);
- Gilbo WWTP—treating wastewater from the Jenin City and Jenin Camp;
- Suriq WWTP—treating wastewater from Ramallah, Beit Jala, and some parts of Bethlehem;
- Shoket WWTP—treating wastewater from Hebron and Kiryat Arbaa settlement.

According to Yarqon River Authority (2015), the South Sharon regional council WWTP has frequent spills that, due to their pollution potential, cause harm to the stream where the effluents are discharged. These pollution hazards are aggravated by faults or damage to the wastewater collection system. This transboundary wastewater management demonstrates a lack of cooperation between both sides and is inconsistent with the principles present on the Oslo II Accord. On one hand, the treated wastewater represents an unconventional source of water for Israel without any similar benefit for the Palestinian Authority. While on the other hand, since the Oslo II accord, the PA has managed to develop few WWTPs.

It is very relevant that, according to Selby (2013), the JWC, an entity created by Oslo II, often operates as a blockage to the accord itself. A thorough analysis of this political matter is, however, beyond the scope of this report.

Decentralized Treatment

There are two main options for decentralized wastewater treatment in the West Bank: collective or neighborhood facilities and on-site household facilities. These types of systems were mainly developed by local or international NGOs and academic institutions for populations that lack sewage collection networks and depend on cesspits for wastewater disposal. Less than 750 of these facilities have been implemented on the West Bank.

Most of these systems have serious operation problems and some do not function at all (PWA 2012). In most cases community WWTPs differ from the expected efficiencies due to poor maintenance, poor operation, and/or lack of financial resources (ibid). Arafeh (2012) estimates that almost 50% of these facilities are not operating or are operating with low efficiency (Figure 6).

These results are consistent with PWA (2012) where it is stated that the quality of treatment in most cases does not comply with the Palestinian standards for treatment and reuse.

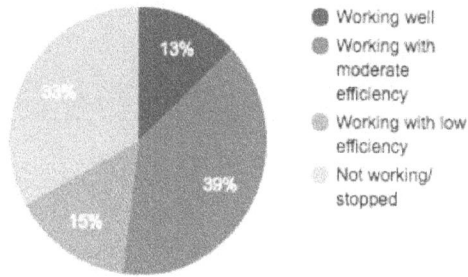

Figure 6: General Status of Existing On-site WWTPs\West Bank. Source: Arafeh (2012).

Case Studies

Overview

In order to compare the sanitation system options in the Palestinian context, two case studies are analyzed. The location and general information of both case studies is presented in Table 2 and Figure 7.

Table 2: Comparison of the General Aspects of Ras 'Atiya and Atouf Villages

Village	Ras'Atiya	Atouf
Inhabitants (present)	1849	400
Total area (dunums)	936	130
Area A (%)	0	0
Area B (%)	33.1	95
Area C (%)	66.9	5

The first case study is Ras' Atiya, a village of 1,849 inhabitants located in the Qalqilya Governorate, in the western area of the West Bank. It is classified as a rural area and the economy depends mainly on the agricultural sector (ARIJ 2013) while having an unemployment rate of a quarter of its workforce (PCBS 2015c). This village has no sovereignty over most of its land, 66.9% of it being area C, with the rest classified as area B.

The second case study is Atouf, a village located east of Tubas Governorate, in the north of West Bank. The population lives off land cultivation and livestock breeding. This village is characterized by scattered population with some clusters of houses. According to the PCBS (2015a), the population is 220 people, whereas the survey made by PWEG (2015) estimates approximately 400 inhabitants. This difference

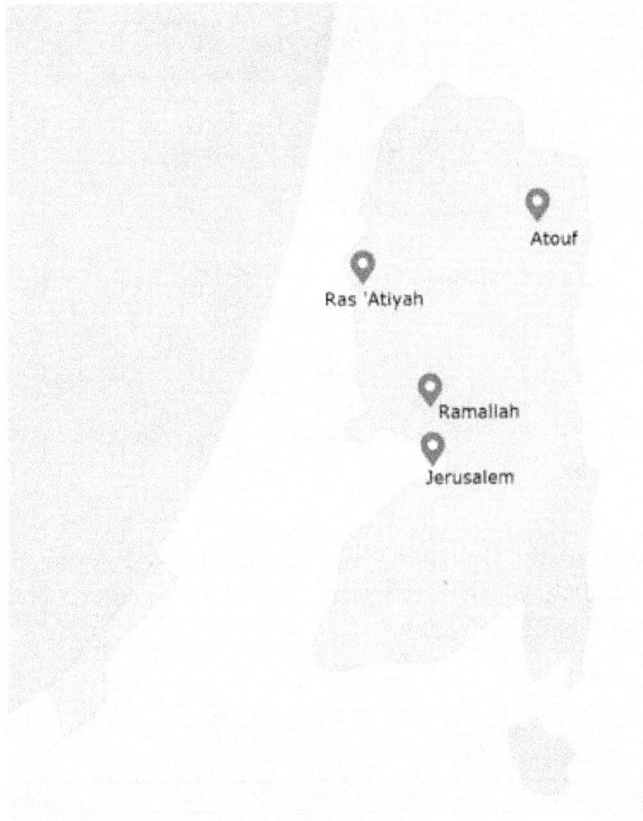

Figure 7: Location of Ras' Atiya and Atouf in the West Bank. Adapted: Free Vector Maps.com.

is likely to be due to fluctuating population as some re-locate in search for better fields to feed livestock. Having 95% of its area classified as "area C," Atouf is considered to be a part of the city and planes of Tamun stretching until the river Jordan (PWEG 2015).

Both of these villages lack sewerage networks. The population relies on unlined cesspits as means of wastewater disposal. Unlined cesspits allow the wastewater to enter into the ground, requiring less maintenance but contaminating the groundwater. When required, emptying of the existing cesspits may be done by wastewater tankers, which discharge the wastewater directly to open areas or nearby valleys with little regard for the environment and public health (ARIJ 2013; PWEG 2015).

Ras 'Atiya—Centralized systems

Water Sources

Ras' Atiya is a village located over the Western Aquifer. The Village Council provides water for its population through the 'Amayer well via the public water networks established in 1995. All housing units are connected to the network (ARIJ 2013).

According to Ras 'Atiya Village Council (2015), the public network was supplied with between 90 and 100 m3/h of water. The pump works 120 h/month which, taking into account the water losses (15%), leads to 'Atiya surpasses the recommended quantity of 100 l/day/capita proposed by WHO. Each cubic meter of water from the public network costs 2 NIS (0.5€).

The village also has 55 individual household rainwater harvesting cisterns and 3 water reservoirs: two with 200 cubic meters capacity and one with 50 cubic meters capacity (ARIJ 2013).

Existing Sanitary Conditions

The use of unlined cesspits facilitates microbiological pollution in the aquifers. According to a communication from the Palestinian Health Ministry, provided by the Village Council to PWEG, the Western Aquifer already shows signs of contamination in the Ras 'Atiya area (Palestinian Health Ministry 2013).

Proposed solutions

In order to provide safe and adequate wastewater management to the population of Ras 'Atiya, a Master plan for the separate sewer network was created. With 2035 as the project horizon, it assessed the possibility of connecting this projected network to the existing sewer network in Habla, a nearby city. Being a separate sewer system, the proposed solution intends to convey only wastewater, excluding storm water runoff.

The proposed drainage system (presented in Figure 8) takes into account these characteristics, the existing constructions and possible urban expansion. It consists of four main lines, connected to three different manholes from Habla's network. Lines A and D encircle the whole village, and lines B and C follow the main roads that cross Ras 'Atyiah, and flow to Habla.

The proposed network encompasses almost the total of population in Ras 'Atiya. Taking into consideration Ras 'Atiya's characteristics, it is expected that most of the pipelines will have a diameter of 200 mm.

The design period for this project is 20 years. The design and previsions of population growth, and evolution of the consumption patterns, are considered for the year 2035.

While the current water consumption for Ras 'Atiya is 164 l/c/d, it is expected to reach 175 l/day/capita by 2035. For the wastewater generation, it is assumed that

Figure 8: Proposal for the wastewater drainage lines in Ras 'Atiya sewer system

85% of the consumed water is disposed of in the sewer system, amounting to 140l/day/capita in 2015 and 150 l/day/capita in 2035.

Investment and Operation and Maintenance Cost

The total length of the proposed sewage network in Ras 'Atiya is approximately 5.6 km of which 5.1 km is unplasticized polyvinyl chloride (uPVC) pipes and 500 m is black steel pipe. The investment cost of the proposed network is estimated to be around 503,800€. The sewage network would require operation and maintenance personnel, both skilled technicians and unskilled labor professionals. The Ras' Atiya council would be responsible for carrying out this task, at an estimated cost of 2,360 € for equipment and 1,650€ per month for personnel.

Atouf—Decentralized Systems

Water Sources

Atouf is located on the northeast of the West Bank, and relies on the Eastern Aquifer as its main water supply. This community suffers from a lack of safe drinking water and depends on an irrigation network for agricultural uses. The water is sourced from an artesian well in the village of Alfara and has excess of iron, making it unsafe for human use. For daily water consumption, people use rainwater harvesting cisterns and buy water from tanks at a higher cost than regular network water distribution. Even with these costly resources, only approximately 60% of the village population enjoys permanent water supply, from the artesian well. Nevertheless, it was expected that 92% of households would be connected to the water supply network by the beginning of 2016 (PWEG 2015).

According to a survey conducted in Atouf by PWEG, the estimated per capita consumption is of 62 l/d (0.5 m3 per household) for domestic use and a total of 100 m3/day for crop irrigation per farmer (PWEG 2015).

Existing Sanitary Conditions

The use of cesspits pollutes groundwater and water collected in domestic cisterns. As the rainwater harvesting cisterns are underground, wastewater percolates and gets mixed with the collected water, contaminating it and making it inappropriate for human consumption.

The survey undertaken by PWEG found that there is separation between gray and black internal wastewater networks, however the nontreated gray wastewater is used for irrigation of trees around resident's households, directly and without prior treatment (PWEG 2015).

Proposed Solutions

In order to equip the entire community of Atouf, West Bank, with household gray wastewater treatment solutions, it was proposed the construction of 25 modified septic tanks (MST) and 25 household gray WWTPs (GWWTP), for up to 16 people each. The implementation of the studied solution it will depend on the fund availability.

The design period of GWWTPs is 15 years. This takes into consideration an increase in the population using the GWWTP and an increase of water consumption due to expected improvement of living conditions following the installation of a water network in Atouf (PWEG 2015).

The system is based on the separation of household black and gray water. The blackwater is conveyed by a 6" pipe to a MST, as shown in Figure 9. The graywater is treated in the GWWTP, as shown in Figure 10, and reused in both protected and intensive agriculture, a greenhouse, or in open agriculture. In some houses in Atouf, plumbing fixtures might be changed in order to separate gray and blackwater streams (PWEG 2015).

The septic tank receives the graywater from the house through a 4" diameter polyvinyl chloride (PVC) pipe. The wastewater flows into the septic tank, with a retention time in the septic tank of 1.5 to 2 days. The GWWTP plants are constructed using concrete or/and hollow bricks. They include anaerobic treatment and filtration after which water is pumped and stored until it goes to the irrigation network (PWEG 2015).

Figure 9: Sketch of the Modified Septic Tank (MST) Source: PWEG (2015)

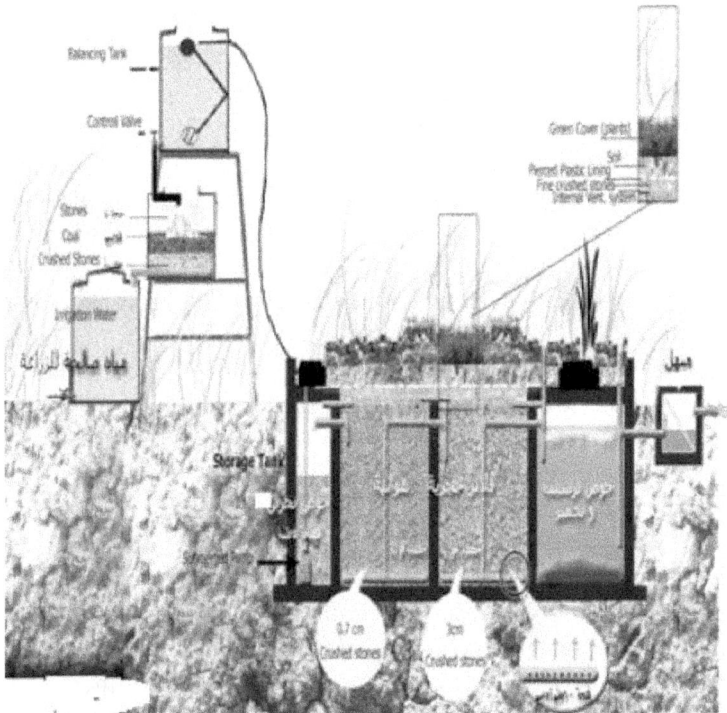

Figure 10: Sketch of the Gray Wastewater Treatment Plant (GWWTP) Source: PWEG (2015)

Investment, Operation, and Maintenance

The estimated investment cost is approximately 62,400€ for the 25 MSTs and 91,000€ for the 25 GWWTPs. The beneficiaries will be asked to contribute to the implementation of the project financially or in kind. Contributions from beneficiaries will be sought, but based on previous experience it is unlikely that all beneficiaries will wish to contribute. In order to maintain the project scope and objectives, contributions will be voluntary.

The proposed system is low technological, therefore no complicated maintenance procedure is needed. For the MSTs the on-going maintenance of the tank and soakage field is mostly the responsibility of the house owner or occupier. The owners should ensure that the ventilation opening on the septic tank is kept clear and the tank is desludged every 15–20 years. For the GWWTPs, the maintenance is also undertaken by the beneficiaries and includes the daily cleaning and removal of solids that are suspended on the screen of the inlet manhole and the scraping and removal of grease and fat, if any, from the first tank. The beneficiaries still have to assure continuous electricity supply to the plant and assure that the pump is working at least twice a week (PWEG 2015).

Conclusions and Recommendations

Regarding the sanitation scenario in OPT, it is clear that the existing WWTPs are insufficient to guarantee good environmental and public health conditions. There are serious operational and maintenance problems and most systems are obsolete. All infrastructures for wastewater management existing in the OPT depend on international donors, and this international presence acts as a catalyzer for the development of this sector. Although it seems that foreign aid may also develop, the apparent tendency of short and medium term planning is not ensuring sustainable O&M taking into account the Palestinian reality.

Due to the geopolitical situation in the OPT, decentralized systems are, in theory, a good option and have been extensively used throughout the whole West Bank. These systems have mostly been implemented by NGOs. This type of solution depends greatly on the willingness and awareness of the owners of the households and managing entities. Previous studies suggest that due to lack of maintenance most of the existent decentralized systems both at community and household level are not functioning in a satisfactory fashion.

The fact that OPT does not ensure the treatment of its own wastewater, this water flows beyond the border of the OPT, making it necessary for Israel to include these streams of wastewater into their own WWTPs. The cost of this treatment is allocated to the OPT, transforming this considerable wastewater volume into an unconventional source of water that is used solely by Israel. However, the systematic reuse of treated wastewater will be essential to meet OPT's water needs in the near future.

This transboundary wastewater management demonstrates the lack of cooperation between both sides and goes against the principles present in the Oslo II Accord. Since the signing of the accord, the Palestinian Authority has managed to develop only the Nablus WWTP. Furthermore, it seems that entities created by the Oslo II, such as the JWC, may operate as a blockage to the accord itself.

The case study of Ras 'Atiya is an example of a transboundary wastewater management system where the wastewater is treated at an Israeli WWTP. This fact implies that the Palestinian population will lose its rights over the treated water. Geopolitical constraints do not follow the topography, leading to the only possible solution of proposing the connection to nearby Habla, not crossing into area C. A sewage master plan that aims to eliminate the use of cesspits that are currently polluting the groundwater is proposed.

For Atouf, the proposed solution is based on a decentralized on-site system at household level. These systems are usually the best solution for very disperse localities such as Atouf, especially given its geopolitical situation (areas B and C).

Besides the centralized versus decentralized debate, in transboundary situations water reuse becomes a sensitive issue. Whenever there is centralized transboundary wastewater treatment, there is a risk that one of the parties involved may lose rights of its treated water. This type of situation should be identified and managed through bilateral agreements. This is especially relevant in cases where all parties require this unconventional source of water to meet the water minimum requirements for either present or expected populations.

It may also be concluded that interim agreements must be taken cautiously whenever the existent diplomatic relations are volatile. Finally, agreements on transboundary water issues should be based in cooperation and goodwill, respecting equally all parties involved and should rest on diplomatic dialogue.

Acknowledgments

The authors would like to thank Cristina Branquinho for all the support and the opportunity to participate in the TransBasin Project. They cannot fail to mention FFCUL in Portugal and Arava Institute in Israel, especially Clive Lipchin, for all the logistic support. Finally, this project would not have been possible without all the team at PWEG.

References

Abu-Madi, M & Trifunovic, N 2013, 'Impacts of Supply Duration on the Design and Performance of Intermittent Water Distribution Systems in the West Bank', *Water International*, vol. 38, no. 3, pp. 263–282. doi:10.1080/02508060.2013.794404.

Almasri, MN & McNeill, LS 2009, 'Optimal Planning of Wastewater Reuse using the Suitability Approach: A Conceptual Framework for the West Bank, Palestine', *Desalination*, vol. 248, no. 1-3, pp. 428–435. doi:10.1016/j.desal.2008.05.084.

Amnesty International, 2009, 'Troubled Waters – Palestinians denied fair access to water – Israel Occupied Palestinian Territories' <https://www.amnestyusa.org/pdf/mde150272009en.pdf>.

Arafeh, GA 2012, *Process Monitoring and Performance Evaluation of Existing Wastewater Treatment Plants in Palestinian Rural Areas/West Bank*. M.Sc. Thesis, Birzeit University, Palestine.

ARIJ 2013, *Ras 'Atiya Village Profile (including Ras at Tira & Wadi ar Rasha Localities)*, Applied Research Institute, Jerusalem.

Bdour, AN, Hamdi, MR & Tarawneh, Z 2009, 'Perspectives on Sustainable Wastewater Treatment Technologies and Reuse Options in the Urban Areas of the Mediterranean Region', *Desalination*, vol. 237, no. 1-3, pp. 162–174. doi:10.1016/j.desal.2007.12.030.

Boavida, S, Pinto, M, Salvador, T, Hind, M & Neto, S 2015, *Centralized and Decentralized Wastewater Systems in the West Bank—Prospective Lessons for Other Contexts*, Ramallah. (not published)

Charbonneau, L & Nichols, M 2012, 'No Palestinians Win De Facto U.N. Recognition of Sovereign State', *Reuters*. Available from: <http://www.reuters.com/article/us-palestinians-statehood-idUSBRE8AR0EG20121201>.

Chenoweth, J 2008, 'Minimum Water Requirement for Social and Economic Development', *Desalination*, vol. 229, pp. 245–256. doi:10.1016/j.desal.2007.09.011.

Howard, G & Bartram, J 2003, 'Domestic Water Quantity, Service Level and Health', *World Health Organization*, pp. 1-39. doi:10.1128/JB.187.23.8156.

Israel & PLO 1995, Oslo II Accords (*Interim Agreement on the West Bank and the Gaza Strip*), Washington, DC. <http://www.mfa.gov.il/mfa/foreignpolicy/peace/guide/pages/the%20israeli-palestinian%20interim%20agreement.aspx>.

Israeli Ministry of Foreign Affairs n.d., 'The Israeli-Palestinian Interim Agreement-Main Points', Available from: <http://www.mfa.gov.il/MFA/ForeignPolicy/Peace/Guide/Pages/The Israeli-Palestinian Interim Agreement - Main P.aspx>.

Jewish Virtual Library 2015, 'Israel International Relations: International Recognition of Israel, Available from: <http://www.jewishvirtuallibrary.org/jsource/Peace/recogIsrael.html>. [30 December 2015].

Weinberger G, Livshitz, Y, Givati, A, Zilberbrand, M, Tal, A, Weiss, M & Zurieli, A, 2012, 'The Natural Water Resources Between the Mediterranean Sea and the Jordan River', Report, Israel Hydrological Service, Jerusalem.

Palestinian Health Ministry 2013, Letter from the Palestinian Health Ministry to Ras 'Atiyah Village Council.

PCBS 2015a, 'Localities in Tubas Governorate by Type of Locality and Population Estimates, 2007--2016', Available from: <http://www.pcbs.gov.ps/Portals/_Rainbow/ Documents/tubs.htm>. [29 November 2015].

PCBS 2015b, 'On the Eve of the International Day of Refugees, Available from: <http:// pcbs.gov.ps/portals/_pcbs/PressRelease/Press_En_IntDyRef2015E.pdf>. [1 January 2015].

PCBS 2015c, *Palestine in figures 2014*, Ramallah—Palestine. Available from: <http:// www.pcbs.gov.ps/Downloads/book2115.pdf>[12 December 2015].

PWA 2012, *Annual Status Report on Water Resources, Water Supply, and Wastewater in the Occupied State of Palestine 2011*, Ramallah, Palestine. Available from: <http://pwa. ps/userfiles/file/تقارير/Annual\nWater\nStatus\nreport\n2011.pdf>.

PWA 2015, *2014 Water Resources Status Summary Report/Gaza Strip*, Ramallah, Palestine. Available from: <http://www.pwa.ps/>.

PWEG 2015, *Osprey Community-Level Greywater Scale-Up*, Al Bireh, Palestine.

Ras 'Atiya Village Council 2015, Meeting with the Council.

Selby, J 2013, 'Cooperation, Domination and Colonisation: The Israeli–Palestinian Joint Water Committee', *Water Alternatives*, vol. 6, no. 1, pp. 1–24.

Shreim, DA 2012, *Environmental Assessment and Economic Valuation of Wastewater Generated from Israeli Settlements in the West Bank*. M.Sc. Thesis, Faculty of Graduate Studies, An-Najah National University, Nablus, Palestine.

Shuval, H 2007, 'Meeting Vital Human Needs: Equitable Resolution of Conflicts over Shared Water Resources of Israelis and Palestinians' In 'Water Resources in the Middle East, Israel-Palestinian Water Issues – From Conflict to Cooperation', First Edition, ed. H Shuval & H Dweik, Springer, Jerusalem, pp. 3-16.

The International Solidarity Movement 2014, Available from: <http://www.ism-france. org/analyses/La-recherche-des-colons-disparus-a-mis-en-lumiere-la-profondeur-de-l-occupation-de-la-Cisjordanie-article-18980>.

Tilley, E, Ulrich, L, Lüthi, C, Reymond, P & Zurbrügg, C 2014, *Compendium of Sanitation Systems and Technologies. Development*, Second Revise Edition., Swiss Federal Institute of Aquatic Science and Technology (Eawag), Dübendorf, Switzerland. doi:SAN-12.

U.S. Department of State n.d., 'The Oslo Accords and the Arab–Israeli Peace Process', Available from: <https://history.state.gov/milestones/1993-2000/oslo>. [26 November 2015].

World Bank 2004, *West Bank and Gaza—Wastewater Treatment and Reuse Policy Note*. World Bank, Washington, DC. <http://siteresources.worldbank.org/INTUWM/Resources/westbank.pdf>.

World Bank 2015, 'Data—West Bank and Gaza', Available from: <http://data.worldbank.org/>.

Yarqon River Authority 2015, 'Pollution', Available from: <http://www.yarqon.org.il/drainage/pollution/>. [9 December 2015].

Zeitoun, M & Warner, J 2006, 'Hydro-Hegemony—A Framework for Analysis of Transboundary Water Conflicts', *Water Policy*, vol. 8, no. 5, pp. 435–460. doi:10.2166/wp.2006.054.

www.ingramcontent.com/pod-product-compliance
Lightning Source LLC
Chambersburg PA
CBHW081721270326
41933CB00017B/3245